Blanche Roosevelt

Victorien Sardou, Poet, Author and Member of the Academy of

France

A Personal Study

Blanche Roosevelt

Victorien Sardou, Poet, Author and Member of the Academy of France
A Personal Study

ISBN/EAN: 9783337778149

Printed in Europe, USA, Canada, Australia, Japan

Cover: Foto ©Thomas Meinert / pixelio.de

More available books at **www.hansebooks.com**

VICTORIEN SARDOU

*POET, AUTHOR, AND MEMBER OF THE
ACADEMY OF FRANCE*

A PERSONAL STUDY

BY

BLANCHE ROOSEVELT

OFFICER OF THE ACADEMY OF FRANCE

AUTHOR OF "LIFE AND REMINISCENCES OF GUSTAVE DORÉ"
"LIFE OF LONGFELLOW," "VERDI," "THE COPPER QUEEN"
ETC. ETC.

PREFACE BY

W. BEATTY-KINGSTON

*Some lives in peaceful meadows flow;
Like brook that steals from hidden glen,
Their tranquil days ebb to and fro,
Their actions "'scape the mark of men."
Far more would I the fiercest strife
Engage, and strike for good or ill;
Who has not warred knows naught of life:
Fate conquers man, man fate through will.*
" First Poems " : BLANCHE ROOSEVELT

LONDON
KEGAN PAUL, TRENCH, TRÜBNER & Co., LTD.
1892

TO

𝕿𝖍𝖊 𝕯𝖊𝖆𝖗 𝕸𝖊𝖒𝖔𝖗𝖞

OF

FRANC B. WILKIE

(POLINTO)

IN ADMIRATION OF HIS RARE GENIUS, IN RECOLLECTION

OF HIS FRIENDSHIP, AND WITH GRATITUDE FOR

HIS ENCOURAGEMENT—MY OLDEST

LITERARY FRIEND

FROM HIS FAITHFUL FOLLOWER

BLANCHE ROOSEVELT

PREFACE

ALTHOUGH, as I have been assured, the function of blowing one's own trumpet is not absolutely distasteful to some eminent personages in the world of art and letters, there are others, to my personal knowledge, who experience an unconquerable reluctance to perform upon that instrument, however importunately they may be solicited to do so by hosts of admiring friends. This is why I, in its author's stead, am writing the preface to this booklet. The purpose of these introductory lines is to set forth Blanche Roosevelt's qualifications for fulfilling the task she has undertaken, not to trespass upon

the literary ground she has taken up
as a biographer of contemporary celebrities.   To the English public there is
a good deal to be said, more or less
new and interesting, about Victorien
Sardou, who in this country is tolerably
well known as a dramatist, but not at
all as a man.   Hitherto no memoir of
this distinguished playwright has, as
far as I know, been printed in our lan-
guage.   Miss Roosevelt has prepared
one which consists mainly of personal
narrative and anecdote immediately
derived from its subject ; of matter,
in short, that has never heretofore
been given to publicity.   This work
has been built up on a foundation
identical in all essential respects with
that which underlay her biographies of
Longfellow, Gustave Doré, Carmen
Sylva, and Giuseppe Verdi, each of
which, so to speak, was suffused with

the personality of its illustrious subject, while bearing the impress of its author's vigorous individuality.

These were the secrets of their indisputable charm: that Blanche Roosevelt knew, and knew well, the persons about whom she wrote; that she is gifted with a Boswellian memory, singularly retentive and exact, which enables her to reproduce the style as well as substance of her interlocutors' verbal statements; and that she is capable of describing what she has seen with peculiar felicity of expression. In respect to its profuse display of these enviable faculties, and of the poetic temperament with which bountiful Nature has also endowed "la belle Américaine"—the epithet was Victor Hugo's—her "Life of Gustave Doré" is one of the most remarkable and attractive books of the past decade;

and it is high, but by no means unde-
served praise of her biographical sketch
of Victorien Sardou, to say that it is
entitled to rank " with and after " that
admirable work, although designed and
executed upon a much smaller scale.

I may be permitted in this place
to briefly summarise Miss Roosevelt's
special qualifications for undertaking
the task embodied in this volume. She
has for several years been privileged
to count Sardou among her intimate
personal friends; has been a frequent
visitor at his house, and has enjoyed
many opportunities of listening to his
brilliant talk and interesting reminiscences of an exceptionally eventful
and adventurous youth. Her first
meeting with him took place at the
hospitable table of Victor Hugo, in
whose house, during the later years of
the venerable poet's life, she was a

favourite and ever-welcome guest. There, at different times, she became acquainted with the leading lights of the contemporary French schools of *belles lettres* and the plastic arts; with Arséne Houssaye, Jules Claretie, François Coppée, Guy de Maupassant, Barbey d'Aurevilly, Alphonse Daudet, Joseph Peladan, Catulle Mendés, Paul Bourget, Meilhac, Halévy, Tourgénieff, Gustave Doré, and many other poets and romancists of the day, who cordially recognised her claims to literary distinction, and associated with her on terms of frank and genial comradeship. Her place among Hugo's habitual *commensaux* was at the right hand of her illustrious host, whose admiration of her prompted him—on a memorable occasion, recorded by Arséne Houssaye in his brilliant preface to the French edition of "Gustave Doré"—to address

her as "The Beauty and Genius of the
New World." When this supreme
tribute of appreciation was paid to
her by the greatest poet of France
she was a girl of seventeen, and, according to Houssaye's graphic description
of her appearance, "lovely with every
loveliness; her fair hair rippling with
sunshine; her blue eyes as deep as the
sky, beneath their dark lashes; tall,
slight and supple as a reed; her profile
one that might have been designed by
Apelles or Zeuxis." A few years later
the Académie Française confirmed Victor
Hugo's judgment of her literary abilities
by creating her one of its officers. It
is scarcely necessary to observe that this
high distinction is seldom conferred by
the "Immortal Forty" upon native
authors of the female sex, and still more
rarely upon foreigners. Even more:
Blanche Roosevelt was the first Ameri-

can authoress to be decorated by the French Academy.

Perhaps no stronger recommendation of this book can be preferred than the assurance—which I am authorised to tender to its readers—that, having been submitted to M. Victorien Sardou in its present form, it has secured his hearty and unqualified approval. He has indeed defined it as " the most curious and intelligent study of himself and his works that has ever heretofore been produced." To this pronouncement— " praise from Sir Hubert Stanley "—I have nothing to add, save the expression of my belief that its justice will be generally acknowledged by the press and the public.

In literary and dramatic circles on either side the Atlantic it will be learned with interest that M. Sardou is collaborating with Miss Roosevelt in

the dramatisation of her justly celebrated novel " The Copper Queen," an
English version of which will ere long
be produced upon the English and
American stage.

W. BEATTY-KINGSTON.

CONTENTS

VICTORIEN SARDOU

A PERSONAL STUDY

THE world wants to know all about its celebrated men and women ; what they are, where they live and how, what they eat and drink, the part they play in everyday life ; and, having talents beyond the ordinary, how much, besides, of the ordinary everyday man and woman. This is not curiosity, but interest. What would we not give to have had a page from some gossiping neighbour who had personally known wise Omar ; known of his loves, his wine, his roses ; a page from one who

had seen Dante and fair Beatrice
walking in the vales of amber Arno;
to have had one word from Tasso as
he mourned the cruelty of the house of
d'Este, or the trivial fond record of
some goodly neighbour who had drank
a friendly posset with Shakespeare and
Shakespeare's love,—sweet Ann Hatha-
way—and yet none can unfold such
pages.   There are many men, however,
before the world to-day, not greater
than the past masters, but whose lives
in this busy epoch are of the deepest
interest, and who will bear the same
relation to future generations as their
great predecessors bear to the present.
Among others, Victorien Sardou, member of the French Academy, poet, dramatist and author, recently before the
public with his plays of "Cleopatra"
and "Thermidor," a remarkable man in
the annals of any time, and one whose

life and career cannot be without interest to whomsoever appreciates the final triumph of genius over poverty, evil fortune, and dire despair.

If you know Paris well, you must know the ancient Quartier St. Antoine —that portion of the city rich in historic interest—where, could it speak, every paving-stone would cry out with a voice from the historic past; a district of wide streets, old-fashioned squares, antique palaces set in quaint old gardens, protected by grim, sentinel-like walls; that in their impassability and solidity have been witnesses to some of the greatest scenes in France's history; long quays fringed with tattered book-stalls or shops; the Quai des Célestins, where witty Rabelais has a plaque consecrated to his memory, and where the march of modern progress and commerce has obliterated neither the spirit nor form of the dim long-ago. This quarter is still sacred to the eager tourist, the old houses are hallowed to the memory of illustrious names, their walls have seen the light of illustrious eyes, and their wide gateways have resounded to the footsteps of many, how many, of France's most illustrious dead. Flowers have bloomed in the old gardens for wearers whose very names are a perfume from a fragrant past; whose lives belong to the world, and whose memories, like hidden streams silently stealing from mountainous causeways, have flowed onward with resistless impulse to join the great ocean of life and immortality and progress.

The old Quartier St. Antoine was divided up into sub-quarters, among others the Quartier St. Paul, the old Hôtel St. Paul, first known to history as the Palace and Gardens of the Kings of France ; and in the ancient plan of the city we see that this demesne comprised a portion of the Quai des Célestins, and extended beyond the Place de la Bastille, to the Barrière du Trône ; ever memorable for the Revolution of 1848, and for that greater page stained by the name of Robespierre and the fatal guillotine. Later, the King's Gardens were divided into streets, each bearing a name with reference to its former state : Rue Beautreilles (literally street of the beautiful trellis), Rue des Cerisiers, Rue des Noisettiers, and, most quaint of all, I remember a streetlet whose name from an etymological point of view is most curious. In old French it was styled " Rue de Pute y Musse," in more modern French " Fille s'y cache," and at the time of the Revolution " Fille s'y cache " was condensed into "Rue du Petit Musse," a name, I think which it bears to this very day.

At that period this was the Parisian Haymarket, a street outlawed to virtue, and a general rendezvous for corruption and vice; a corner held in horror and shunned by all the good people living in its immediate neighbourhood.

While the century was still in its adolescence a certain Professor Sardou and his wife lived in a charming house set in a quaint garden, in the Rue Beautreilles, and on the 5th September 1831 Madame Sardou presented her husband with an heir — Victorien Sardou, the greatest living dramatist. One more added to the memorable names which adorn France's galaxy of greatness to-day, and have, since many a day, been renowned in the annals of France and of French dramatic art.

Good Professor Sardou, in his

modesty, little dreamed that his son's name was destined to become, not alone a household word in his native country, but a household word wherever literature, the stage, or drama have found shrines and enthusiastic followers ; but so it was, and, as all the world knows the genius, many would like to know the man ; as all the world knows his artistic life, many would also like to know his home life ; to read one of those cloud-pages which publicity rarely opens, but which, when opened, exhale a sweeter perfume than any flower of fame. Being privileged, I open the pages ; being persistent, you may peruse them.

Sardou once said to me : " Never be afraid of slow commencements ; have your characters fully, solidly planted, engrafted as it were into the soil. Balzac and your Walter Scott and

Dickens knew how to do that "; and in virtue of the dramatist's own words, in order to appreciate the development of so rich and varied a genius, we must go back to his earliest days, when he trundled his hoop with other lads in Père Beaumarchais' garden at the corner of the Place de la Bastille ; a boy at school, when he pattered around the old Quais des Célestins, d'Orsay and Voltaire, studying with eager curiosity the advertisements on the illuminated kiosks, or thumbing with childish reverence the musty volumes heaped in picturesque confusion on the low-lying shelves of the riverside book vendors.

Monsieur Sardou, senior, whose residence has been transferred to Nice, was, and is, a most remarkable man.

At the time of Victorien's birth he was a leading professor in one of the leading Parisian Colleges, author of several elementary classics, a man of deep historical research and a certain literary attainment, also famous for editing an edition of Rabelais, the envy of even Lacroix—better known as the Bibliophile Jacob. Sardou's wife shared his talent in much, and his taste in everything; their home was simple; they lived very retired, but whenever they went out or received, they frequented the choicest wits of France; hence Victorien was rocked by birth, so to speak, in a literary and artistic cradle. He once said to me:

"My father knew everything and went everywhere. I do not so much remember great people at our house, but I never heard other than great names spoken, other talk than talk of the popular authors and celebrities of the day; and I remember that I was never happier than when I went to play in Père Beaumarchais' garden. Not alone because he was a dear man, but I suppose because he was Beaumarchais."

As a lad his precocity and memory were fabulous ; he absorbed, he never learned ; his lightning-like quickness and retentiveness were the marvel of family friends and neighbours. Add to this a curiosity without limit, a faculty of observation approaching witchcraft, a sensitiveness more in character with a romantic growing girl than with a clever, highly strung youth, and you have a picture of the dramatist from his early years to that latest florescence when he dreamed of becoming, not an author, but—do not start—an Æsculapius : one of the famous Parisian medical brigade who have also an academy ; rivals of that

noble forty among whom Victorien
Sardou is one of the most brilliant
and universally renowned.

Sardou studied medicine and cultivated hospitals and dissecting tables ;
he attended lectures and clinics and
côteries ; frequented Professor This,
the celebrated nerve man, and Professor That, the renowned phthisis
man ; attended the soirées of Madame
la Professeur This, and danced at the
cotillons of Madame la Professeur
That ; but all to no avail. If people
felt ill they did not send for him, and
if they died—they could not blame him.
The blackest of poverty stared him
chronically in the face ; he worked on
hope, but starved on despair, and his
unique solace was studying the old
Greek drama ; but one day it dawned
upon him that he preferred the dissecting table of ancient history to that of

human ills and human anatomy. He gave up medicine and became historian and student ; working in those fertile meads, embroidered by the genius of a Michelet, a Thiers, or a Taine.

Only those who have known the sting of bitter want can fully appreciate the agony of the intellectual student's career. The eager brain, the famished body, the long night watches and hideous nightmares, the struggle to make both ends meet, to keep body and soul together, the continual battle with poverty, pride, ambition, hope, and despair.

Sardou's young life was such a struggle ; and the terrible ordeals to which his ardent receptive nature was subjected—in spite of himself—have left their mark. As we must crush the rose to get the attar, so there are human flowers which thrive best under misfortune. Sardou possessed a valiant soul; one of those resisting plants which flourish in adversity, which blossom on the dew of tears, and bloom only to their fullest beauty under the sun of never-failing courage and ambition.

He did not give way; the more he had to work against, the harder he worked, and every new trial fell like a pointless dart against the steel armour of his resistance. He determined to be some one, and realised that the bridge which connects greatness and nothingness is knowledge. Although he daily passed the old Théâtre Molière in the ancient square of St. Paul's, and was familiar with the artists and authors of the day, he never once thought of becoming a playwright; but in order to prosecute his studies gave lessons in history, philosophy, and mathematics.

He wrote articles for dictionaries, dailies
and even medical journals; he wrote
essays and essayed serious stories; and
one novelette, " La Perle Noire," found
its way into the hands of a good, even
discriminating public. He toiled day
and night with the dogged perseverance
which ever has been and is one of his
most eminent characteristics; no pains
were too great to take; he was never
behindhand in any promised work, and
ever striving to improve his mind; to
garner up such a store of miscellaneous
information as few, even of the most
noted erudites, possess to-day. He
thus laid the foundations, not alone of
that fame and fortune so justly his due,
but of all the envy, jealousy, and ridiculous exaggeration afloat in France,
which repeatedly, though vainly, assails
one of her most brilliant and versatile
sons.

In the midst of these enforced classical studies, Sardou began to feel the quickening of that dramatic instinct which has brought to life such splendid and noble creations. He adored the play, but was equally devoted to the opera, and, speaking of the latter one day, said :

"Ah, don't talk to me of music; that is one of my passions. I remember, a long time ago, when I went to the opera, not in box or stalls, but right up in the gallery, to hear the 'Huguenots' or the 'Prophet.' I delighted in Meyerbeer. The seats were four francs apiece. I had probably pawned my best coat to get there ; but there I was, and I never think of those costly evenings without remembering how I enjoyed them, and felt a certain sense of gratification that I have never experienced since."

"And now," I replied, "other students pawn their best clothes to sit in the gallery or on the roof, not to hear Meyerbeer, but Sardou."

"Mais naturellement," he said, laughing, "c'est ainsi que va le monde."

My mind went back to the past, to the old Rue Lepelletier Opera House.* I did not see the successful author in white cravat and regulation swallow-tail, but a poor lad in working jacket and Dantesque cap, leaning over the gallery rails, happiest among the gallery gods, an enthralled student, forgetting the long day of worry, fatigue, and care; forgetting that he had not dined, even though his best cutaway was at "my

---

* Napoleon III. was going to this theatre the night of the famous Orsini throwing of bombs. The house was burned in November 1873, the very day on which Count de Chambord threatened to come from Versailles, en Rio, with the famous but fated white flag of the Bourbons.

uncle's," oblivious of all and everything but the splendour of the scene, the music, the lights, the public; filling his soul with the inspiration of the divine; inspired, shabby and ignorant, yet dreaming of the day when he should be something. or somebody; wearing in his bosom the rose of youth and youth's happiest, dearest illusions.

Then, the opera finished, I could see him going back to his modest home, humming a gay tune as he crossed the Pont d'Orsay, happy as he supped on a biscuit and glass of syrup and water, happy and hopeful as he seized pen and paper and scribbled off that first play, " La Taverne des Etudiants," brought out at the Odéon, and destined to be, not his first success, but his first most complete, irremediable failure.

This was in 1854, and Sardou was so disgusted and disappointed that he

B

determined never to write another play ; happily for himself, however, and the world at large, this determination did not hold good. In 1858 he married Mlle. de Brécourt, and found in this charming companion a panacea to many of the ills of existence. He took courage, and again thought of the theatre, but life was a sore struggle with poverty, chagrin, disappointment, and overwork. His supersensitive nature was beginning to feel the effect of these constant and rude shocks that a precarious existence entails upon the lives of genius ; blows which fell on all sides and began to undermine both physical and moral force.

Ordinary people cannot live in the world and be impervious to its contact and its contamination ; those alone can do this who have the poet's nature, the resource of its ideal ; the eternal background of beauty and delight, which makes a palace of the most sordid hovel, and gardens of Paradise of the meanest courtyard. It must be a very strong character that can resist the daily communication with all that is mean, much that is abasing, and more that is distasteful, without the original sweetness of the nature becoming soured. Sardou's bright hopefulness was quenched, and the wit that enchanted friends and family soon sharpened to a satirical blade which cut right and left, as sure and fatal as the scythe which sweeps the dewy meadow of its earliest blooms.

Still, in many respects the Sardou of to-day is the same Sardou. With all the old nervousness, the quick sympathy, the brilliant wit, the ready tear ; a good lover, a good hater ; a man of extremes, the most loyal of friends, the most bitter of enemies ; anything you like, eager, intense, interesting and interested, but never indifferent. He rarely alludes to his past experience, but if anything brings it forward, he speaks with the utmost naturalness and unconcern. There is nothing pontifical about Sardou ; his simplicity is delightful as agreeable, very unlike many successful writers of the day, who cross the street when they see the old friends who knew them in poverty, and read all of Tom Hood excepting the lines : " And I would that the coats of my stomach were such that my uncle might take."

Sardou is of such a striking individuality that after a few moments in his presence you realise at once that you are before a man and a mind which have lived through the most terrible of ordeals. To the romantic impression-

able lad, running all over Paris with
verses in one pocket and plays in
another (a second Frederick the Great
on the eve of more than a seven years'
war), to this lad, in his impressionability
and facile enthusiasm, it were easy to
predict his future character ; the contact of the world, the absorption of
worldliness, hopes fled and dreams
vanished ; the bloom brushed from the
grape and the perfume fled from the
flower. The old story of idealism
versus realism, when for long years the
latter dominates ; until the world seems
one vast sea of commonplaces covered
but by the floating wrecks of vanished
dreams ; themselves dreams of dreams,
shades of shadows, already become a
vague mass of that distant vague horizon which despair calls destiny and
fatalists designate as the future.

One day we were speaking of the

deceptions sensitive youth knows, of
the shattering of our idols, of the ruth-
less hurling from their fair pedestals of
gods whose names to us are as the
canopy of heaven.   M. Sardou himself
gives the keynote to his somewhat
cynical character, condemned by the
many, understood by the few.

"Ah," he cried, "to whom do you
speak of deceptions?   My life has
been one long deception, spent in seeing
my idols shattered and my gods de-
throned.   I remember the first great
illusions I ever had.   I was an enthusiastic boy, running all over Paris with
plays in my pocket that no manager
wanted—I don't wonder, they were
bad enough then—I was so fond of
reading, that in the streets, or on tops
of houses, I was always devouring some
work—one of the classics or of the
works of George Sand, then at the

zenith of her fame, and one of my pet
idols. I thought of her; I dreamed of
her; I scarcely ever hoped to know
her; but I hoped some day at least to
see her. One morning I went to the
Odéon with a play rolled up in my
hand—not accepted, of course; the
stage manager told me they were
rehearsing one of George Sand's pieces,
that the stage was full, and Madame
Sand there, superintending the stage
setting. 'Madame Sand!' I screamed.
'Oh, let me go on the stage; let me
look at her, let me go near her; find
me a place somewhere—do!' I was
wild with excitement. My idol! I
was to see her at last. As I went on
the stage—very timidly, of course,
and as awkward as any school-boy—I
saw a large, not ill-favoured woman,
looking like a cook, rolling up cigarettes,
and lolling in a large arm-chair. The

cigarettes I noticed particularly, as the regulations were very severe, no one being allowed to smoke on the stage. I thought to myself, that is some old duenna or the manager's stage cousin ; but imagine the shock when I heard and realised that she was George Sand ! That blow, however, was slight. Her appearance was the first shock, and you must admit that, for a poet to see his idol looking like a cook and smoking one cigarette after another, was not exactly the dream, the goddess, his fancy had pictured. The rehearsal went on. At a certain point there was a lull, and one of the machinists, or firemen, was obliged to cross the stage. He had but just started when Sand caught sight of him ; she stopped short with the cigarette she was rolling, she turned from the manager, then speaking to her, and her eye followed the *pompier* out of sight ; when, instead of answering the manager's question, with a bland smile she murmured, ' Il est bigrement bien fait ce gars là ! '

" Illusion ?   Another ?   Pray, listen. If there was one man in the world I had a feeling of affection for, that man was—well, one of our greatest poets. His life, his exaggerations, his personality surrounded his genius and his beauty with that Byronic sort of halo the very idea of which dazzled me.   I thought if I could ever know him I would be perfectly happy ; I would be willing to walk miles barefoot for the sole hope of looking upon him ; but what chance had a poor struggling devil like myself of ever meeting the most brilliant poet of the day ?   Sought after in Court and salon, a being almost a myth to his best friends, and the one man all Paris at that time was raving over and bowing down to ?   From having so often looked at his picture I knew his face and form by heart, and I really loved him with the romantic passion of a student, who worshipped such mind, genius, and fame. Early one morning I was on my way to the Théâtre Français ; it was pouring with rain.   I had just reached it, when I observed a man sheltering himself, leaning against the sides of the walls— the pillars, you know—near the Palais Royal.   This man was emaciated, haggard, shabby ; he was so intoxicated that he could scarcely stand, and once I thought he would reel into my very arms.   As I approached I saw, to my horror, who it was, and naturally looked with all my might a mingled look of curiosity, interest, sorrow, and chagrin. He returned my gaze, swaggered to one side, cocked his hat, and began : 'What are you staring at ?   Who are you and

what do you want ? Move on, curse
you ; move on !' Each word prefaced
with the vilest oath I had ever heard,
and each phrase followed by a string of
vituperation enough to make a Billings-
gate *habitué* shudder. He raved on in
such a torrent of abuse that I thought
he had lost his senses, and could scarcely
credit the evidence of my own.

" At last I could stand it no longer ;
I recoiled, gasping, 'Not the great
poet !' ' Idiot !' he screamed, 'whom did
you expect it was ?' And, with a dreadful hiccough, added ' Poet ? *Je le
crois bien.*" Then, loftily, drunkenly,
touching his hat, with another choice
selection from his choice vocabulary,
he reeled, swearing, away, and was
soon lost in the crowd of the street.
That was the only time I ever saw my
idol, the greatest poet of his time—
a being whose very name to me had

been the synonym of all that was great, glorious, and enviable. *Mais— que voulez vous ?* "

"Yes," I added : " *Sic transit gloria mundi ;* " and Sardou, in turn smiling, said : " *Je le crains bien, que voulez vous ?* "

PERSONAL APPEARANCE

I HAVE remarked a curious coincidence. Three women, probably the greatest in brain-power of the century, actually resembled each other, not alone in form, but in feature. Need I name George Eliot, George Sand, and Madame Viardot? Victorien Sardou also strikingly resembles three great persons—Dante, Voltaire, and the First Consul.

At twenty years of age he looked so like Bonaparte that it was ridiculous; and Arséne Houssaye showed me a little silver statuette of the Emperor, which I thought and said must be M. Sardou dressed for a *bal masqué*.

After the seasons that have waned and faded, in spite of the fatigue and cares of brain-work, the face has at times a Napoleonic expression, a Dantesque, a Voltairian expression, which adds a strange character to this characteristic physiognomy. No one could even glance at Sardou and not recognise in him a personage. He has that indefinable something about him which attracts, and one and all turn a second time to look at a man of such marked personality.

He is of about medium stature, of a very slight physique, very spare, very active, very eager. Everything about Sardou is alive; his gestures are perfectly graceful, his speech is graceful, his walk is graceful; but naturally his face exercises the greatest attraction. A broad, square forehead, crowned with masses of long and still lustrous black hair, scarcely threaded with a tinge of grey. His face is still clean shaven; the mobile mouth, which denotes keenness, firmness, and tenderness, is veiled by a fine ironical expression, only changing when he smiles: a rare, seductive smile, which shows all his kindliness, and would be charming even in a woman who wished to charm. His eyes are dark grey, large and sparkling; they light up with every expression of his face, and long before he speaks indicate his humour; in short, the whole face is one of intensity, eagerness, and intelligence. Sardou is not one of those sleepy geniuses who sit like tame cats for hours, then suddenly spring some extraordinary thing upon you. He is not only alive, but seems the very incarnation of life, of readiness, of being. He is very remarkable at his rehearsals, but he is quite as remarkable when reading one of his scenarios, or skeletons of plays, which, by the way, are very far from being skeletons, as these first studies are in themselves almost complete plays, the flesh of composition already more than covering the framework of bone and sinew.

Sardou is a perfect actor ; takes every part and illustrates every one of his characters with such versatility and vigour that the illusion is quite complete. You may laugh and you may cry with him, and never know how it came about ; indeed, the stage in him has lost a great actor.

It is usual to lend to celebrities virtues as well as vices which they do not possess, and because Sardou is a close man of business and looks well after his affairs, many imagine that the milk of human kindness does not overflow his veins ; that he is hard, cold, and unimpressionable ; but those who know him know the contrary. Should you hear otherwise, remember Byron's answer to his wife, ever complaining of what those around her said of her husband : " Madam, has it never struck you that you do not live amongst my friends ? " Sardou hates injustice and imposition ; he has not the facile generosity of Dumas, senior, who borrowed twenty francs of an impecunious friend's servant, and tipped her with the whole sum as she showed him to the door, observing : *"Je n'ai pas de monnaie, tiens !"* But Sardou is sympathy itself ; many and many are the artists he has helped, and many another not in the artistic world.

Poor Virginie Dejazet, who had squandered fortunes and was always without a halfpenny, ever and anon

experienced to the very last how true
a friend the dramatist was; an old
woman, dead to the scenes of her former triumphs, interred, as it were, before
she was dead, playing half an hour at
some morning performance, a fleeting
apparition at some charity entertain-
ment, just because she had been
Dejazet; running into the provinces to
show the younger generation what a
comédienne of the old school was, drag-
ging her seventy years about as though
they were thirty; struggling to the end,
one fatal illness, and her real last appearance on the stage of life. Besides
the memory left behind her were a
few grateful letters, wherein Sardou was
more than once mentioned, and finally
the flighty Parisian world realised that
generosity does not alone consist in
heading lists of public charities, that
one man who had kept in the back-

ground was the one who had alone been the final stay to old age and dying, decrepid talent.

Sardou's kindness to young authors is proverbial, and many a once obscure scribbler is indebted to him for rank, position, and comfort in the world, spiritual and material. Nine out of every ten who rush into dramatic effort complete their first play and are off to Sardou with it. The maître not only gives advice and wonderful counsel, but arranges, corrects, criticises, suggests, and to some privileged few even shows his own way of working. The amazing *mise en scène* book, a huge volume in itself, which contains scarcely a word of dialogue, is like a general's plan of campaign. Every movement, every gesture, almost every thought that the player is to reproduce, is designated in full—the furniture, the walls, the doors

the windows, all have their rôle clearly
marked out.

This is the most wonderful book I
have ever seen, and shows the trouble
the maître takes over his plays.   It is
an inductive sort of study, and demonstrates, even more than the completed
drama, the perfection of the completed
dramatic scenario.   This scenario, as he
calls it, is an absolutely speaking score ;
and once, when submitting a scene to
M. Sardou, I complained of not finding
some words I wanted.   He smiled
grimly, and said : " Le geste fait naitre
la parole, trouvez le geste, et vous en
aurez même de trop."

He does not spare those to whom he
gives counsel ; on the contrary, his
time, if worth anything, must not be
wasted, and his advice, if to be followed,
must be taken literally and absolutely.
He once raved at me for—well, perhaps

an hour—because I had written something to my mind very fine, but to his
very inferior.

"Ah!" he cried, "you think it is in
that way people write plays? Miss
Jones arrives. Perhaps she comes
from the Arc, or perhaps from the
Tour Eiffel. No one knows anything
about her, her antecedents, her family ;
you drag her in, spring her upon your
audience ; not a preceding word or
gesture from any one leads up to who
she is or what she is, and because she
rattles off a volley of smart words you
think it is all right. She goes off as
she came on, but instead of being
agreeable, she mystifies everybody—
clle déroute tout le monde—and your
play is well-nigh damned long before it
has been either heard or played."

And so he raved on. I did not
dare open my mouth and think it one

instance on record of a woman keeping her tongue, still for—for so very long a consecutive time. His remarks were scarcely flattering in one way, but to have had such a lesson in the art of writing for the stage I would have stood much—but very much—more. My only regret is that the world could not have heard him : had there only been a shorthand reporter at the door, or a crafty phonograph in the room, posterity might be richer by one of the most electric, eloquent, scathing, splendid outbursts ever delivered extempore on the art of constructing and writing modern plays for the modern stage.

When he had finished he was all apology, kindliness, sympathy. He said :

" Dickens could never write a play ; Balzac could never write a play ; novelists cannot write plays. If you

could, you would not need to come to
me to help you. Writers will not
understand the terrible mechanical ap-
prenticeship necessary to turn even the
greatest dramatic instinct to account.
The labour must be unceasing, the
effort unending, the self-scrutiny im-
placable ; then, if you do not in the end
show genius, you at least show training ; your play will be well put together ; and we all know that the genius
of modern drama is its construction,
and without that you might as well
expect to write a good piece as to build
a fine house without any foundation-
stones." He added, smilingly : "You
have listened well. Thanks ; but at
one moment your attention strayed.
What were you thinking ?"

" I was thinking of the great Pauline
Viardot," I replied, " and a music lesson
I once heard at her house. George

Sand was on the sofa, and sat near to Madam. After a few weak-hearted passages she closed the pupil's book. The girl seemed in tears."

"That's all very well, Miss," she said, "but don't you think you had better weep at home? It really is not worth while coming here and paying me twenty francs a half-hour to cry."

Sardou: "C'est ça! Nous apprenons tous à pleurer. Mais—ça conte moins chère de pleurer à la maison."

MY DIARY

ON the 2nd of August 1887 I went to visit M. Sardou at Marly. The day was hot, very hot. I found the maître in the garden, storming because two gardeners, told to fill up a cavity at the base of a fine old oak, had spent a day doing the contrary, undermining the finest tree in the park.

" Voyez-vous ? " he cried ; " what the ordinary intellignce is. Within an hour I explained perfectly what these men were to do ; I left them five minutes ; they talked things over, and this is the result. I once felt sorry for servants, especially when their errors caused

them to be scolded by their masters,
but that was a long time ago. Never
fear, water finds its level, and in all my
experiences of life I have never yet
found one human being in an inferior
position above that position ; on the
contrary, they are usually far below
it, and have all they can do to main-
tain even their inferiority before their
world."

I take the following from my diary:
I should call it from my Sardou :—
Only imagine you have before you the
brilliant eyes, the ready, fascinating
smile, the quick, nervous manner, and
clear, sarcastic voice of the maître.
Sardou is so bright, and seizes upon
the points of a thing so instanta-
neously ; his repartee is so happy that
wit seems to flash from his body.
After one of his brilliant sallies you
some way expect to see his coat

sparkle, or diamond dust shine on the small black *toque* set on the small Dantesque head.

After the gardener episode we began talking of his play, to quote himself, "for the great Sarah." He questioned me of my own work, and I said, "I am studying Poe at present." He then began about our national glory, and simply raved over Poe's genius and literary skill.

"One night, long ago," Sardou said, "a poor student, on my way home, I stopped, as usual, at the book-shop on the Quai, when I ran across an old review-magazine with 'The Purloined Letter' in it, translated from the original, without the author's name, but with the name of the translator. I was wild to find out who had written the original. I was so struck with the intricate and almost miraculous reasoning evinced, especially in those remarks about the Cobbler playing and being too small, that the story ran incessantly in my mind for a very long time. Some time afterwards Baudelaire's work appeared, and put all Paris in an uproar. Imagine my surprise to find among the collection my delightful ' Purloined Letter.' Baudelaire was a nobody—absolutely unknown—and he startled the world with his Edgar Poe translations." (*Poey*, as the French pronounce it.) And speaking of the " Purloined Letter" reminds me that "Les Pattes de Mouche," Sardou's most brilliant effort, and one which will remain with the classics, must certainly have been a little inspired, in part, by the marvellous and intricate story above named.

During the conversation Byron's name came up, and Sardou cried, " Ah ! mon Dieu, that reminds me of La

Guiccioli ; a long time ago she was my
neighbour. She was the Marquise de
Boissy, and Boissy always presented
her as ‘Madame Guiccioli, my wife ;
but the Guiccioli, you know, *the very
same* bonne amie of Lord Byron.’
Very funny ! and if he thought that any
body present did not understand that
fact, he would hunt them up to explain
it fully to them. La Guiccioli was still
fair, and wore a blonde wig, an imitation
of her tresses of the olden time ; not so
rich as the real Venetian red, which was
once her greatest beauty ; but this hair
was curled just the same, and she seemed
to think she appeared just the same.

"She talked—they talked—very freely
about Byron ; and one day she said to
me : ‘ I’m going to publish his letters,
the entire correspondence, but you know
it is very shady—il y a des choses biên
scabreuses—*mais* des choses the world

must not see.' 'Naturally,' I cried; 'and these are the very ones that the world in general, and I in particular, want to see.' So we arranged to dine on Saturday at her house, and go over the whole correspondence. She added in the coolest way in the world : ' Boissy is ill, dying ; he can't last long ; anyway, we won't be disturbed on Saturday ; I feel that he is going, and once gone, there is no reason why I should not publish Byron's letters at once. Before his death, you understand, the family— so foolish, Boissy's family are so idiotic, they object to my saying anything more about Byron's letters; but as the Marquis is so near the end, I may as well get at the correspondence now.'

"Well, Friday came, and Friday night—the night before I was to dine— Boissy was breathing his last. The following morning, Saturday, he was dead. The next week, when I began to think about the correspondence, the Marquise told me that Boissy's family were giving great trouble, that she did not know what to do; however, she was going to publish the letters. She did publish them later, and there was absolutely nothing in them. A book that was absolutely inept, and anything but an honour to the memory of a great man. Ah! poor Byron, he had no luck at all. I was dying to see that correspondence, and had I got hold of it, I surely would have counselled her not alone to keep copies, but to print those letters exactly as they had been written. You see the letters of so great a genius are public property—they cannot be tampered with; and these should have been given to the world intact as he wrote them, or they should not have been given to the world at all."

Speaking of Byron, Sardou mentioned some of the poet's dramatic works, and gave me an opportunity of asking about his own play which he was then writing (since called " La Tosca ".). "Don't talk to me," he said, " of my works ; I am absolutely beside myself."

He flung thirty or forty pages of MS. about, written in his spider-like impossible hand. " These," he cried, indicating the manuscript, " represent six weeks' work, condensed into this." He showed several pages of copy, " of which " (he smiled a grim smile) " remain but two."

Across from top to bottom, with two strokes of the pen, he had wiped out the whole composition.

" Not cancelled ? " I cried. " Oh, what a shame ! "

" Much greater shame to have left

them," he remarked coolly; "they were absolutely worthless"—he smiled another quiet smile—"but I am used to that; only it is rather hard to spend weeks, day and night, in midsummer weather, to find out that I am but an imbecile. 'And now," he said, " I have stopped short. I'm writing this play; I have the names of all the principals, but I can't find a name for my heroine. The woman is called Floria, but I can't invent a surname for her."

I suggested maliciously, " That which we call a rose, by any other name "——

" Oh, stuff and nonsense ! " he interrupted, good-naturedly. " The name ? —the name ? ' What's in a name ?' Why, everything. Le nom, voyez-vous, c'est une chose terrible. I'm haunted night and day. I've gone through every family name in Venice from the

D

Doges down." Then he began count-
ing off one after the other alphabetically
on his fingers, and, with his eager intensity, cried :

" The name I want must be short ;
it must suit her ; it must be like, very
like the character, and it must end in *a*.
Floria—a : there you are. I can't get
it, and until I do I am absolutely un-
done."

The accidental quoting " a rose by,"
&c., started us on Shakespeare, and to
say that Sardou does not like the great
master would be saying a great deal.
That he criticises him is to acknow-
ledge but the truth, and of the plays
" Hamlet " took its share of condem-
nation.

Naturally I bridled, and said : " You
are a great erudite, a great student ; but
while you read the master in French,
you only know a French Shakespeare

and a French Hamlet." The idea
seemed to strike him ; still, he retorted :
" But the dramatic scenes are the same,
the dramatic action is the same."
" Pardon me," I replied, " they are not
the same ; the action is not the same at
all. Shakespeare's Hamlet is not good
enough for France. Two better writers
have introduced a scene in the second
act. I think the second act enough
to make the Anglo-Saxon hair rise.
Mounet-Sully is so mad when the play
begins, that had he been in Denmark,
or anywhere else, he would have been
suppressed by the authorities, and
Shakespeare never would have written
the tragedy. What would you think
were we to tamper with your Corneille,
your Molière, your Racine, your Scribe,
&c. One sample of the French trans-
lation of Macbeth is ' Out, brief candle '
—*Sortez, courte chandelle.* Another

(M. Richepin's latest) in 'Macbeth' :
one of the witches says, ' I go,' &c.—
'*Fiches moi le camp.*' " Need I say
Sardou laughed ?   " But," he said, " I
read the original, and I appreciate the
difference."

There has been so much discussion
about what Sardou has said of Shakespeare, that I not only subjoin a conversation held with him on the 21st of September last at his house in the Rue Général Foy, but a letter on this very subject.

" You speak of Shakespeare," he said,
" and arrive just in time to see a copy
of the letter written to the *Daily Telegraph* on this very question.*   I shall

---

* M. SARDOU'S CLÉOPÂTRE.

September 24, 1890.

To the Editor of the Daily Telegraph.

MONSIEUR,—En réponse a un article du *Daily
Telegraph*, daté du 27 Août, vous trouverez bon que
je vous addresse deux mots de rectification.

L'auteur se serait épargné des frais d'eloquence

be glad when people are tired of talking about me, what I have done—above all, what I have never thought of doing, of publishing interviews which have never taken place, and of propounding theories that I have never even thought of discussing. They then give my supposed opinions upon accepted classics, and say that I said this, that, and the other.

---

inutiles s'il avait pris le soin de verifier tout d'abord l'exactitude de ses assertions. Il donne comme certain que la " Cléopâtre " qui doit etre crée prochainement par Sarah Bernhardt est une adaptation de celle de Shakespeare ; c'est une erreur. Il eut été plus sage d'attendre l'apparition de la pièce pour parler en connaissance de cause que d'affirmer cette prétendue adaptation a seule fin d'écrire un article malveillent, qui, portant a faux, n'a plus de raison d'être.

On pense bien qu'il n'a pas négligé de rééditer à cette occasion ma fameux phrase sur Shakespeare : " Qu'il n'a pas le moindre talent ! " Mais il a oublie de prouver que je l'ai réellement dite. Il ne suffit pas que l'on m attribué une sottise, pour qu'elle soit a mon actif. Je ne suis pas, il est vrai, des idolâtres qui admirant Shakespeare sans réserves, et je me

" Some person has made a statement that I declared Shakespeare had no talent—a thing which I might have said, but which I did not say.   No one with a grain of common-sense could speak of Shakespeare's talents.   He was a genius ; he was Shakespeare ; and that ends it.   Notez bien que je ne suis pas de ces fanatiques qui admirent tout dans un génie et qui

---

permets de trouver que son statue usurpe en plein Paris la place qui conviendrait mieux a celle de notre Corneille ; mais de la au jugement que l'on me prête, il y a loin ; et je mets votre redacteur au defi de citer un ecrit de moi, que qu'il soit, ou figure cette enormité.

Il n'a même pas l'excuse de la bonne foi ; car j'ai protesté publiquement contre cette phrase l'égendaire ; et s'il pretend que ma protestation lui était inconnue, je lui repondrai qu'un journalists qui se respects n'a pas le droit de connâitre l'accusation et d'ignorer la défense.

Agréez, Monsieur, mes salutations distinguées.

V. SARDOU.

PARIS, *September* 1890.

insistent que tout génie soit perfection. Il y en a du bon Shakespeare et il y en a du mauvais ; même votre Angleterre a reconnue cela, il a même eté question, si oui ou non il avait écrit de certains œuvres ; tant qu'il y a de difference entre l'un et l'autre. Par exemple, l'on veut me soutenir que les Contes d'Hiver, Deux Gentilhommes de Verona, Troilus et Cresside—que ma foi est bien curieux—et d'autres vaillent Otello, Jules César, Macbeth, ou Romeo et Juliette ? Ah, par exemple non ; ca ? Jamais de la vie. C'est comme les gens qui veulent me soutenir que Racine, Corneille, et Molière, n'avient jamais écrit une mauvaise page ; c'est de la betise tout pûre. Nous savons tous que Le Cid est une merveille et que Surena est toute autre chose, etc. etc., enfin sans en finir." Which words should, I think, settle the vexed question of Sardou *v.* Shakespeare, to use a little more French, à tout jamais.

He also said : " I am not willingly a critic, but my profession makes me one. I am obliged to discriminate. I am still a student, a working man ; I cannot follow things and people blindly. I must have my eyes open and know what I am about ; and in reference to a conversation above quoted as 'to the fitness of men and women for the tasks they set themselves, so much do I love men and women in whatever walk of life they may be who do their work thoroughly ; so much do I loathe these slovenly, careless creatures who undertake everything and accomplish nothing; for the former I have a real, veritable affection, while the latter I can never look at. There is no medium with me ; people are either capable or incapable,

trustworty or untrustworthy ; and that
sums up all human nature.

"I do not care in what walk of life,
however humble the person, I reverence
the conscientious worker.

"I remember at the theatre— at the
Porte St. Martin—there was an honest
fellow named Camus, whom I actually
loved.   He was a property-man, always
ready, always cheerful ; all his heart and
soul in his work.   He would listen to
the rehearsals, and evidently absorbed
scraps of conversation relative to the
piece—what would be required, what
would be easy, and what would be diffi-
cult to find ; and the next day, without
a word to any one, would come quietly
up to me and say, 'M. Sardou,
I heard you mention you wanted
such and such a thing.   I had a bit of
time yesterday on my hands ; I hunted
about ; I came across this.'   And per-

haps a lamp, or a fork, or spoon ; and he
would hand me the object.   Perhaps a
nothing, worthless in itself, but just the
one thing wanted to fit harmoniously
with some elaborate scene.   Now, that
is what I call doing work for work's
sake.   His sole ambition was to bring
anything to bear upon the needs of his
position, and I honestly loved that man.
He is dead now, poor fellow, died a
short time ago ; yet every time I go to
the theatre I miss something, and when
I look around and find that his vacant
place is filled by another, I know what
that something is."

Then Sardou gazed unconsciously toward the window, and I gazed unconsciously toward him.   Camus's rank
was humble, but the poor property-man
will never be forgotten.

SARDOU AT HOME.

Another slip from my Diary.—Christmas Day, 12 *a.m.,* 1890. *Paris.*—I have been again reading to M. Sardou from the little sketch of himself I have made, and when we came to the part about his rich residences he burst into a little laugh. As the children say, his face smiled all over ; then he jumped up—(what a man !—he is as active as quicksilver)—he jumped up and fetched an old engraving of old Paris, called "Le Pont de Notre Dame," and said, simply :

"My houses ! I will tell you of one residence not so rich as those you have

described.   You see this quay, the Seine,
the church, &c.?   This was old Paris,
and called le Quai des Fleurs.   In 1852
I lived with another medical student in
a mansarde in this very house (pointing
out a block of quaint, curious build-
ings): and you may judge of the size
of our garret when I tell you it was so
low that neither of us could stand up
in it with our hats on, without touching
the ceiling.

"You see the bridge" (again indicating the place); "well, the whole Seine
at that point was studded with flower
booths, and when, in the early morning,
we opened our windows, the air which
stole upwards was our sole breath of
fragrance.   It was delicious, delightful.
Leaning from our casement we could
see right and left the long sweep of the
Seine shining in the sunlight, and, as
far as eye could reach, many a beauti-

ful old building—alas! a thing of the
past—quays freighted with their moving
mass of humanity, the little marts and
the myriad bouquets on the vendors'
richly heaped tables, made the river-
banks one long, lovely, scented garden.

" There was an old woman who had a
little kiosk upon the end of the bridge,
who sold hot potatoes and chestnuts,
and I used to run down early to buy
our, at that time, most sumptuous breakfast—two sous' worth of hot boiled potatoes, one sou's worth of bread, and
one of fresh butter, procured from a
little market stall beside the first flower
booth.   Then I would run home again,
and you may imagine with what appe-
tite and pleasure we devoured our delicious repast. Mon Dieu ! The number of times I did that I never could
tell.

" Now and again my friend went out,

for if one was busy working, naturally the other had to go out for the *déjeûner*. Then we worked like slaves all day, when we had a sort of hodge-podge, God-knows-what kind of eight-sou dinner, swallowed in some Latin quarter pot-house about seven p.m.

"But that is not all about my mansarde. Listen, pray.

"One morning, years afterward, I was breakfasting with my old friend Baron Haussmann * at the Hotel de la Ville (he was then in process of tearing down and rebuilding Paris). Not knowing exactly where we were, I went to the window, and looking opposite, cried '*Tiens!* I know that house—I recognise it ; they are——'

---

* Since deceased, January 1891. The famous architect of the last Napoleonic Empire, who changed, restored, beautified, and to quote the Ex-Emperor of Brazil, Dom Pedro, Haussmanized Paris.

"'What is it?' said Haussmann.

"'What is it?' I replied; 'nothing—only they are tearing down my mansarde. I—I lived there a long time ago, when a poor medical student in the Latin quarter,' and pointed to my old student home. It was being demolished at that very moment. A strange feeling, perhaps of sadness, came over me. How I would have liked to have visited it once more.

"'Had I known of this rebuilding,' I added, 'I would have come——'

"Haussmann interrupted me, and was for stopping them at once, but it was too late. While we were yet looking the roof fell in—my poor old home was no more!"

Sardou's voice trembled slightly, and I thought how like the story of the mansarde was to life. Haussmann shrugged his shoulders, of course, and said what no Frenchman, when he gets a fitting chance, ever misses saying: *Tout casse, tout passe, tout lasse.* But I add, so it is with man. Everything has its day, its end. Our ambitions, our hopes, our joys, our sorrows, our memories, even our regrets—in the morn of life—crown life's fair edifice with what youth thinks an immortal crown; but in the evening the walls totter and fall, until the last becomes enveloped in the smoke of time's fatal fires—that crucible whence arises the mist-hiding present past and future; future present and past.

Sardou is one of the richest dramatic authors living, and there is a vast difference between the humble lodgings of the long-ago and the charming house in the Rue Général Foy; the once regal residence of Marly le Roi, not to mention the magnificent palace of ever-changing Nice, designed by none other than the playwright himself; for our poet Sardou is no mean architect, and adds to archæological, historical and dramatic gifts, that of a draughtsman, than whom there are few cleverer professionals and certainly very few abler amateurs. Sardou designs pictures, costumes, houses, stage scenes, gardens. He has a knowledge of every century and its customs since the flood at his finger-ends.

This was demonstrated in a famous controversy which began with La Haine and was scarcely quieted with Theodora; and all Paris remembers how Mr. Darcel, a professional archæologist, vainly contested the historic correctness of the fork used by Theodora; and in 1882 there was another quarrel about Odette and Phalammena; Mario Uchard being the last to wage war and

E

lose the battle with this terrible and infallible authority, Sardou.

Until six years ago the maître lived in a flat in the Rue de Clichy—a street, by the way, where Victor Hugo lived for many years (at No. 21), and Sardou moved from the Rue de Clichy into the newly named Rue du Général Foy, properly in the Quartier de l'Europe, just above the beautiful church of St. Augustine. Many of the oldest and best families in France still cling to the idea that it is not the correct thing to have a house facing the street, but rather one looking into the courtyard, oftentimes surrounded by a high wall and often enclosed within heavenly gardens of magic and enchanting loveliness. I do not know about the garden; but in this, as in everything, M. Sardou is most correct. His house is on the court, quiet, retired, and a

perfect gem in its rich, harmonious perfection. From the ante-chamber to the
salon the rooms are tapestried with
magnificent gobelins ; every object the
eye falls upon is a fit companion to its
mate, and an open staircase leading into
an interior apartment gives one a passing glance of richly furnished landings
and rare tapestries guarding the doors
to the upper chambers. To the right
of the inner or first drawing-room is the
poet's sanctum, a little low chamber, in
dark harmonious tints, with books all
round, pictures all around, cabinets all
around, and underneath one a row of
boxes labelled like those one sees at a
solicitor's, containing valuable MSS.,
plays, &c., and two desks in the middle
of the room heaped high with a miscellaneous mass of papers ; the second
table faces a stained-glass window,
where the dramatist sits for long hours

and composes. There was one picture in the room I remember : an old bit of a bridge crossing the Seine, some old houses rich in colour and a street well known to the inhabitants of the Latin quarter. I recollect Sardou looking at it once, and as he looked a softness stole over the pale face, and, with his rare, seductive smile, pointing out its accuracy as a picture of old Paris, he said :

"I'm very fond of it ; it brings back the days of my youth."

Sardou is the most methodical man in the world, the most eager, the most intense, the most indefatigable. He gets up at six o'clock in the morning, summer and winter—he will have no laggard about him ; at seven everybody in the house must be moving. He then breaks his fast with a light cup of tea or coffee, and works straight on until eleven or twelve o'clock, when he takes his French breakfast, and, if not interrupted with callers or rehearsals, resumes and goes on till three o'clock, when his day's writing is supposed to be ended. It is then, however, his work really begins—always something to do with his plays : a young actress to coach in an old part, scenery to look after, the stage manager to see about properties, the costumier to see about costumes, and the general manager to go over everything in general. Then comes dinner, a light repast (Sardou is a very simple eater and drinker) : an evening spent at the play, when, if not a first night, the actors are not playing well, he invariably says : " Tell them Sardou is in front," and all slovenliness instantly vanishes. Or perhaps a hurried appearance at some assembly in the great world of fashion. Sardou in principle and politics is a monarchist, and very seldom frequents any other than the society of the old Faubourg, or a few of his literary and artistic intimates. As he said himself, there is no half-work with him. He cannot tolerate the society of nonentities. He is a very simple, silent man ; has a rare head for business ; he makes a few friends, but staunch ; and his greatest happiness is to be in the bosom of his family with his wife and four lovely children.

Madame Sardou was Mlle. Soulié (daughter of a distinguished legitimist and archæologist at Versailles, and one of the honoured and esteemed friends of the princes of the house of Orleans); a fair, sweet woman with a face like a flower, of rare manners and gentleness ; in short, a *très grande dame,* and, if I mistake not, the model in early days of those wonderful dramatic creations—

one of those winning maidens, admitted
by the world at large to be the most
perfect pictures ever framed in the
dramatic gallery of to-day, and of
whom Sardou, with pardonable pride,
says, " As to my young girls, an honest
man would marry any of them." His own
only daughter is a child all grace and
sweetness, and when I first caught a
glimpse of her walking under the trees
at Marly, she came upon me with a
strange, old-fashioned grace, with quite
the manners and mien of a princess in
a fairy tale ; a part of the old château
of Marly le Roi, that superb royal
demesne under whose arching trees
Louis XIV. had often walked ; whose
vast parks and gardens were the
favourite promenade of many a " *belle
dame sans merci*," and now the favourite
walk of the dramatist, his family and
intimate friends.

Sardou was determined to become the possessor of this splendid property; and it is said that the first purchase-money, 25,000 francs, comprised the royalties from " La Famille Benoiton," played at the old Vaudeville Theatre in the Rue Vivienne. The old château of Marly was destroyed during the Revolution; but there still remains the site of the fountain and an ancient column, ruins of the long-ago. It is not to be wondered at, Sardou's love for this spot, for it is one of the most truly beautiful in France.

Marly is situate on a high plateau overlooking the grand sweep of the Seine valley. St. Germain, with its forest and terrace, to the left; Bougival, with its quaint châlets and fair gardens, to the right; with the Seine lying at its feet, cutting the meadow like a broad watered ribbon, or bubbling through the fairy-like wheels that feed the aqueduct and the mysterious fountains of royal Versailles.

Sardou's house naturally is one vast treasure of art and artistic objects. Among other curios there is one of the famous Inquisition instruments of torture ; a most uncomfortable piece of furniture even to look at, the very sight of which, I am sure, would drag from me any confession regarding myself or my neighbours. The master's study is in the middle of the château, on the ground floor, overlooking the garden, commanding a view of the lovely vales and woods surrounding the estate. The room is filled with books and engravings, books everywhere being in the greatest profusion ; in fact, such a heterogeneous mass of papers and copy that the master's lynx eyes alone would be able to ferret out and classify the whole.

The entrance to the château is very imposing—a pair of gates of massive bronze, with a wonderful Louis XIV. railing, and peeping through, on either side, a row of those famous stone sphynxes so admired in the Champ de Mars in 1867 ; and in the garden, gleaming white through the trees, a statue of Christopher Alegrain, which once belonged to Madame de Pompadour. The old fleur-de-lys coronets and monograms of Henry IV. and Marie de Medicis were destroyed ; but a curious column, dating from the beginning of the seventeenth century, Sardou found intact. He had the French and Florentine fleur-de-lys, with the initials of the above named sovereigns, restored, and replaced in their old positions in the garden.

The new house which Sardou is building at Nice, after his own drawings

and designs, overlooks the whole of
that part of the Rivière and the Ile
de Ste. Marguerite whence Marshal
Bazaine made his memorable escape.
It is an immense feudal-looking pile,
with its battlements and Trecento tower,
and occupies so much space that I
scarcely know whether to call it properly
the construction of a castle or the
destruction of a mountain. He spends
much time in superintending the
building of his last and favourite home,
and, to the delight of Nice and les
Niçois, promises to make it his future
winter residence.

SARDOU'S WORKS.

M. SARDOU is a product of the century. He possesses brain, nerve, fire, adaptability, flexibility, patience and perseverance: add to these a will of iron, and one quality, perhaps his greatest, he is a man of progress. He moves with the times; he is alert, concentrated, serious. And how many to-day in any walk of life are serious?

Here you have before you a man whose mind has not run in a groove, who has not cultivated one talent at the expense of all other talents, but who, on the contrary, has employed various qualities to support and prop up the one. A tree is not held to the earth by one root, but fastened by many, each one in its turn shooting out the tennæ, the which, widespread, sustain the superficial whole. Remember that the world has known a Michel Angelo, a Cellini, a Da Vinci, and a Shakespeare. Hence, when in Sardou's plays one remarks the cleverness of certain scenes, or suggestions, or intricate mechanical technique, that the ordinary dramatist would never have dreamed of, recollect the reason of this completeness, and also recollect that if there be exception the rule can scarcely hold good. Had he so wished, the jack of all trades might have mastered at least one, and now we arrive at the great secret of dramatic art.

When you see and remark certain (to you) anomalies in a stage character, do not declare this, that, or the other to be unnatural. The fact is, that, on the stage or off, men and women are seldom natural. We attribute to them virtues, through our ideality and vices, through our indifference. But if a man whose whole life and life's study has been the cause, effect, and aftermath of humanity, holds the mirror up to nature that you yourself hold up, recollect that even this mirror shows but a bounded part, and nature alone furnishes the living quicksilver for her own indescribable limitless self.

Sceptical Pilate said: "What is truth?" And who of us may dare pretend to know his neighbour, even his most intimate friend? The caprice of brain, the subterfuge of circumstance, the ruse, the trick of habit, civilisation and its monstrous necessities, have aided one and all to dominate, almost nullify, original matter. On the stage, listening to a sudden outburst or noticing an unusual situation, you may declare such or such a character would not have acted in such a way or have put himself in such or such a position; but, believe me, you would declare wrongly. The dramatist who evolves all, everything, from the magic crucible of a cultivated brain, makes up the great human whole after rule, rhythm, and natural law. Reflect and admit how much more likely it is that you in your untutored honesty should be mistaken, than he, a professed student in his native element, aided by his immense experienced art.

Perhaps that is why M. Sardou occupies the first place in dramatic art to-day. One may dispute his genius, his talent, his taste, but none may dispute his exceptional position; and, whatever he may be considered in

France, the world at large unhesitatingly places him at the head of the French dramatists to-day. In 1887 he was elected, almost unanimously, to fill the chair in the French Academy left vacant by Joseph Autran, the poet author of " Les Poëmes de la Mer " and " La Fille d'Eschyle "; and in spite of a whirlwind of opposition of talk, *pro* and *con.*, defeated both M. D'Audiffret Pasquier and Lecomte de Lisle, the renowned poet and most perfect versifier in France. On the 7th June 1887 the ballot was decided in favour of M. Sardou. He took his seat a year later, pronouncing, as is the custom, an eulogy on his predecessor, conceded even by his opponents to be one of the most brilliant and masterly speeches of the day.

Sardou has achieved his brilliant position by dint of a singularly pure

dramatic temperament, by histrionic
abilities of the highest order, and an
historic mind, rare enough in these
modern days, stored with matter which
would not shame the greatest of erudites ; an indefatigable capacity for
consecutive labour scarcely paralleled
among writers. and workers of the
century.

Putting aside all natural qualities, I
should unhesitatingly style Sardou the
greatest dramatic artisan of the epoch.
I use the word in the proper sense,
meaning a labourer or builder ; a man
who makes form out of matter, who
mosaics the tiniest bits into that which
becomes a great whole. Who but he
can find those ingenious situations,
those startling attitudes and audacious
chimeras which abound in his works?
For the mind is not merely ingenious,
but the workman is such a master of

his craft that he begins by knowing his own weaknesses and ends naturally by playing upon the weaknesses of others. In dramatic scenes he seems to delight in urging his *dramatis personæ* to the very verge of the possible—a hair more, and they would reel into the gulf of the bathetic and impossible.

This note is particularly observed in " La Famille Benoiton," in " Divorçons," " Nos Intimes," " Dora," and " Maison Neuve " ; and I must not forget " Rabagas " and " Les Pattes de Mouches," certainly our author's most brilliant works, destined, and most justly, to remain classics of the French dramatic style. I do not speak particularly of " Divorçons," written with the late De Najec, " Belle-Maman," with M. R. Deslandes, or, latest, " Cleopatra," in collaboration with M. Moreau. I well remember almost the first words

M. Sardou ever said to me in reference
to this very subject: " Quant a moi je
n'aime enfanter que les énfants a moi ;"
and it is a noteworthy fact that every
play he has brought into the world by
himself has been so healthy and beautiful a child that even a Spartan mother
would have delighted in such offspring.
Witness the last, " Thermidor," a model
of genius, art and mechanical artisan-
ship.

It is impossible here to touch upon
all Sardou's works. The world knows
his successes. I should like to point
out the good points in his so-called
failures, " La Haine " and " Daniel
Rochat." I speak especially of " Daniel
Rochat," which, in spite of its fall at
the Comédie Française, with " Odette,"
paved the way of the great modern
movement in France, the law of divorce.
And the subsequent comedy " Divor-

çons," in spite of its riskiness, formed a notable pendant to the original intention of the plays.

As to " La Haine " (performed first at the Gaité in December 1874), it is a repulsive drama, but absolutely remarkable. It deals with the wars of the Quattrocento, between Guelphs and Ghibellines and Charles of Bohemia, in Siena. The picture of the old city, the furious combats, the dishonoured Cordelia, the hero, Tribune Orso, the Bishop Azzelino, Giugurtha Saraceni, the raging crowds, the frantic soldiery, the tempestuous mobs, are like pictures, not alone Italian, but as faithful to life as Italy herself. Here we realise the fundamental basis of Sardou's art, modelled on the old Greek dramatists —meaning action, action, action, than which no higher praise can be awarded any dramatic author.

Those who saw " La Haine " will
never forget it ; and in spite of its terrible, even revolting theme, I think
any one caring to turn over the pages
of the musty past could find no greater
profit or pleasure than to go back
to the Siena of the fourteenth century, and live again those strange
wild days, Italy's history of the long-
ago, in this wonderful curio, " La
Haine."

The non-appreciation of " La Haine "
was a blow to the author, but did not
dampen his historic ardour. " La
Haine" was intended, according to
Sardou's letter, to be an historical
companion to " Patrie," the character
of Cordelia, in its humanity and femi-
nineness, to apologise for the vengeful
and extravagant Dolores—one of Sardou's wonderful women, an intrigante
and traitress, but even as intrigante and

traitress far from the ideal dreamed by the master.

Writers, however, cannot do as they will with their characters. People in books and in plays are like people in everyday life; some you care to see and some you do not care to see; but friends, neighbours, strangers, they force themselves upon you; they come uninvited; they go unattended; they worry your life out of you; they try to pass off the most vulgar curiosity for the most intense interest; they invade you body and soul; they know all you have done, all you are doing, and all you are going to do; you murmur, you struggle; helpless, you finally succumb: these beings have their own way. Thus, in plays and romances, as in everyday existence, you begin with the ideal and end by accepting the inevitable. Sardou, with a fertile brain,

vivid imagination, and redundant fancy,
has still been handicapped by himself.
He has done all he could do to eman-
cipate his genius, to isolate his literary
life ; but time, place, and circumstance
have often willed otherwise ; and if
there be dull points and unexplained
harmonies, they are the result of the
eager fastidiousness of a mind which
grasps too much of a dramatic horizon,
ever limitless, and which at its best
must fall short of the creator's glowing,
splendid, and immense ideal.

Sardou's versatility is demonstrated
by a repertory as varied as curious.
We have the grandest height of tragedy, the thrilling sensation of the
comedy-drama, the delicate wit and
pathos of pure comedy, with at times
the irresistible humour of low comedy
and broad farce. " Candide " and " Les
Premières Armes de Figaro " were given

successively at the old Théâtre Dejazet, as were "Monsieur Garat" and "Les Près St. Gervais," music by Lecocq—a most delicious comic opera ; and "Les Gens Nerveux" was played at the Palais Royal. To the Gymnase belongs the honour of having brought out the famous "Pattes de Mouches," since transferred to the Comédie Française, its proper place ; "Piccolino," music by Giraud, was produced in 1861, "La Perle Noir" in April of 1862, and "Les Gauches" in November of 1862. At the Vaudeville, "L'Ecureuil" was presented under the pseudonym of "Cart"; and I must not forget "Nos Intimes" in November 1871, one of the most popular of Sardou's creations and most extraordinary successes. Among others we must cite the universal "Famille Benoiton," "Les Vieux Garçons," "Nos

bons Villageois," " Maison Neuve,"
" Seraphine," " Patrie," " Dora," " La
Dévote," " La Haine," " Fernande,"
" Le Roi Carotte," with Offenbach's
perennial music ; and the 1st of Feb-
ruary 1872, the never-to-be-forgotten
representation of " Rabagas ": " Rabagas," a political satire with real personages on the stage—the Gambettas
and so forth of the Palais Bourbon and
the Parisian boulevards. A whirlwind
of discussion, *pro* and *con.*, followed it ;
all Paris ran to see it ; and not alone
France, but every civilised country,
talked about it. Sardou was again
asked to write for the Comédie Française, where he had previously made
an unsuccessful effort with " Le Papil-
lon." He prepared the scenario of
" Daniel Rochat," subsequently slated
through political intrigue and journal-
istic jealousy. Bear in mind that

Sardou is a liberal monarchist, living under a republican government; and undoubtedly the last-named is one of the reasons to which one may attribute, not alone the failure of "Daniel Rochat," but the never-ending quarrels, dissensions, and cabals which hold, and still attack, every new venture from this prolific pen. The last work for the Française, "Thermidor," is an illustration of this. It was first called "La Dernière Charette," and, as its name suggests, deals with the last days of the great Revolution. It was written just before the Commune, and after lying away in sandal-wood for two decades, Sardou thought the proper moment for its production had arrived. What occurred is already legend.

But his failures are only as a drop in the bucket compared to his successes; and if I may prophesy, all the former will be forgotten, exterminated, in the triumph of " Thermidor," the new Revolution drama, great beyond any power of word-painting.

From the success of " Dora "—something colossal—we arrive rapidly at "La Patrie," of which work we can only say it will remain, and deservedly, a classic. Then comes those plays best known to the English public—that sequence of wonderful women with names ending in "a "—" Andrea," " Dora," "Fedora," "Theodora," and "La Tosca."

" La Tosca " is so well known to the English public that I permit myself to say here a few words about it.

In these days of electricity and railway travel it would be idle to assume that Italy is an unexplored country ; and yet how often have we seen in drama and romance how little Italy and the Italians are really understood ; even

so recently as in the " Struggle for Life "
we had the pleasure of meeting an Italian diplomatist, an officer employing a
phraseology as Italian as the Boulevard-
Exterieur-Parisian-Argot, in a costume
unknown to Italy of any time, scarce
known to judicial England of sixty years
ago ; but Sardou never falls into these
errors, and only those fully conversant
with Italy, her literature, her people, her
customs and her stage, can appreciate
how truly Italian " La Tosca " is.

The English version, while being
written *secundum artem*, begins by nul-
lifying one of the most psychological
points in the play—the acute religious
sentiment combined with the absolute
moral bluntness which obtains from the
top to the toe of the married woman going to meet her lover, but taking in the
cathedral on the way, enjoying a sort of
pre-remorse as consoling as universal.

The British matron will say that it is
but correct to make " Caravadossi " and
" La Tosca " man and wife ; but the
student who goes to the play to study
a nation, its manners, its customs,
through the characters therein repre-
sented, must regret that the English
adaptors felt themselves obliged to
make a hybrid creature into a Pamela,
and do an amazingly clever dramatist
an injustice as unnecessary as ridiculous.
" La Tosca " coming to meet her lover
within the very walls of the sacred edifice, and with the innocence of a Posilippo
peasant going through a form of wor-
ship, to which her whole life and con-
duct were a living lie, is a study of
nature and skilful rendering of art as
true as nature itself, and could only
have been envolved by Sardou's genius,
culture, and experience. There are
Italians, and they live in Italy ; but

rarely will one ever see one transplanted to foreign soil more complete, life-like, or natural beings than the creations we find in " La Tosca." The Marchese Cicisbeo would have delighted even Byron. "Caravadossi," " Scarpia," and " La Tosca " are not alone absolutely Italian, but absolutely Neapolitan, *et c'est tout dire.*

The second act is the one wherein we find most to criticise. The poet's licence may cover much, and in an historic play we doubt whether any author has a right to transpose history for stage purposes, especially history so well known as that of the infamous Marie Caroline and her disastrous reign in Naples. The scene, however, is very cleverly devised (taking place in Rome, instead of the actual place, Livorno), the queen waiting for dispatches, and La Tosca, the cantatrice,

suddenly interrupted in her attempts to
sing. The cleverness of this scene
surpasses all word praise. The Italian,
high or low, noble or plebeian, is a creature of impulse, disinterested, natural.
If she get in a temper, her head may
go to the block, but her passion must
have full vent.

Any young woman, however, with
behaviour like that of Floria Tosca, in
this scene, would not only, have been
ordered to leave the presence, but most
likely have been put into a dungeon on
bread and water until, as a public per-
former, she had learned that humility
and etiquette notorious of the epoch,
and which even so late as four decades
since, was characteristic during the reign
of King Bomba ; still, knowing, realising
her probable fate, the singer throws
protection to the winds, and the woman
asserts herself in all the supremacy of

insulted dignity and outraged position—
not alone at the Court of Naples, but
throughout all Italy ; and even to-day
any actress, who in a drawing-room
would dare to call a titled courtier an
imbecile, would stand a very fair chance
of having her carriage ordered.   Is this
not clever ?   It would be very skilful
in an Italian dramatist ; it becomes
unauthentic in a French or foreign
writer.

What we must look at in " La
Tosca" is its truthfulness to the life,
country, times, and character it repre-
sents ; and all must admit it to be a
marvellously fine and clever piece of
work.   The third act plays itself—
another instance of Sardou's exquisite
technique of construction ; and here the
English adaptors are not very much at
fault, as it is a question of humanity
and not of etiquette ; whether lover,

husband, brother, or friend, the naturalness of the torture scene comes home to
all, and wrings all hearts alike. The
next, the hideously realistic murder of
Scarpia, for dramatic intensity, is one
of the most extraordinary ever con-
ceived or written even by Sardou ; and
the thrilling last act, where La Tosca
throws herself from the Bridge of St.
Angelo, is a masterpiece of dramatic
handicraft, such as one may alone expect from so experienced a writer and
ingenious a workman as the master.

The next great work was " Cleopatra,"
of which the public heard the result
long before this study was completed.
The only scene in the " Cleopatra "
which is based upon Shakespeare, according to Sardou himself, is the "Scène
des Messagers."

Surely the life of the " Serpent of
the Nile," the times, the manners, are

such that imagination can ever be appealed to, with respect to them ; and the wonder is that we have not had more *Cleopatras!*

I forbear a criticism of " Thermidor," as the world has already heard the play discussed *pro* and *con.* ; and the ludicrous, even painful, treatment it received at the hands of a Théâtre Français public will remain as memorable an event in the history of dramatic art as those scenes and events so faithfully portrayed in " Thermidor " remain the most lively and terrible in the history of France. New York may now judge for herself, and I doubt if any of the master's greatest works will ever have taken a stronger hold on Gotham's playgoers. Although I subjoin some of London's best criticisms on " Thermidor," I must point out two effects—one almost, the other entirely

ignored by the press in general. At
the end of Act Second, where the convent is despoiled and the Sisters are
being taken to prison, a religious
chorus is mingled with the street cries
and rabble's clamour, of such dramatic
intensity that the effect is absolutely
blood-curdling. The faultless nicety of
intonation, the perfect note here struck
by Sardou, not alone demonstrates his
musical ear, but an exquisite culture of
a musical intuition worthy of even a
Meyerbeer. In short, I know of but
one opera to which this scene may be
compared, and all lovers of the "Huguenots" need not be told the one I refer
to. I am not surprised that Sardou
has always been called the god-child of
Scribe and Beaumarchais, but to my
mind not even Scribe himself has ever
surpassed, even if he has equalled, this
extraordinary and miraculous creation.

The second point is the scene where Labussière is going to substitute an unknown person for the victim condemned to the guillotine—all the sympathy is *for the unknown.* It is probably the first time in theatrical or operatical annals that a person unseen —a rôle which plays no part, a creature, in short, who never appears upon the stage, *perhaps never existed* except in the brain of the dramatist—shall have so completely gained the compassion of a not too tender and discriminating public.

Sardou was more struck with the effect produced by this *invisible unknown* yet evidently palpable personage, than any other *moving backwards and forwards* on the living platform of his revolutionary heroes and heroines. With his keen sense of humour, never sparing himself more than another, he said :

" The success of the evening was the rôle played by an individual not on the bills, one who never comes on the stage, whom no one has ever seen, and, when you come down to it, one in fact who has never even existed but as a possible victim—*toute la sympathie du public était pour lui.* In writing my drama, I must confess I scarcely expected this creature to play a *star part,* but such he did, and it was only one more proof, one more striking evidence, of the way an audience may accept certain scenes, and of the strange audience-pulse beating beneath the first-nighter's mantle ; perhaps a more curious testimony still of how an author, even the most experienced dramatist, may gain an effect absolutely ignored by himself until the moment the public judge and pronounce on his work." Sardou thought when he was going to save the life of Fabienne (a being all loved, for one who, to be paradoxical, was a mere chimera, and who even, if existing, could scarcely have an equal claim with her on one's attention) he was doing the right thing ; but, as he has explained, the populace thought differently, and demonstrated, as it always does, that the cause of sympathy, like that of love, has hidden springs, and wells forth only to the magnetism of subtle electric currents and powerful human emotions.

That Sardou has been lucky in his interpreters is acceded. Clever Virginie Dejazet and Fargueil, and lastly, to quote himself again, " La Grande Sarah," are such inspired artists, that to name them, as well as delicious Mlle. Bartet, is to say enough. Sardou may owe something to these gifted artists, but the fact remains, that where an author has humanity for a fundamental basis, and his characters run up and down the whole gamut of human passions, it would need very bad actors and actresses indeed to ruin situations, not only eminently dramatic, but eminently supposable. This last we hold to be the secret of his success.

Sardou is reproached with writing for his century. But why should he not write for his century? Did not Homer, Virgil, Juvenal, Omar, Plutarch, Dante, Machiavelli, with a legion of others, write for their centuries? It may be vastly clever to write a sixteenth-century play in the nineteenth century; but it strikes me as vastly more clever to write a nineteenth-century play in the nineteenth century—where everything is known, where everything has been done, where form as form has given place to fecundity, where there is neither romance, nor mystery, nor chivalry—enthusiasm is below par, and centuries of invention, brilliancy, wit and elegance have been condensed, swallowed up in the great Maelstrom of modern acquirement, achievement and necessity. It is very well to talk about the ancients. Could they have had our electricity and we their learning, no doubt it would have been the acme of human possibility; but to make one's self marked among one's fellows to-day, through the great qualities of the past, seen through the light of this terrible microscopic present, is indeed something to do, and something to be proud of. This Sardou has done, and we are all grateful to him for his efforts to please, to instruct, to amuse; we are grateful for the laughter, for the tears, for the heart-burnings, for the reconciliations, and can only wish him as many happy hours for himself in the future as we have experienced from his plays in the delightful past.

THERMIDOR *

[THE eleventh month of the French Republican Calendar. It commenced July 19, and ended August 17. The Republican Calendar of the French was substituted for the ordinary calendar, dating from the Christian era, by a decree of the National Convention in 1793, after the close of the Revolution, and the 22nd of September, fixed upon as the day of the foundation of the Republic, was also the date of the new calendar. In this calendar, the year, which began at midnight of the day of the autumnal equinox, was divided into

---

* The opposite page presents a facsimile of a cancelled page in MS. of " Thermidor."

twelve months of thirty days, with five additional days for festivals, and every fourth year a sixth.   The months were divided by decades, and the days into ten hours of 100 minutes each.   The names of the months in their order were : Vendemiaire, Brumaire, Frimaire, Nivose, Pluviose, Ventose, Germinal, Floréal, Prairial, Messidor, Thermidor (sometimes called Fervidor), and Fructidor.   The calendar was abolished, and the ordinary one restored, by Napoleon in 1806.]

The action of the play of " Thermidor " covers the space of one day only, but one day in the " Reign of Terror." The story is that of a young girl whose only crime is having been a daughter of the aristocracy, and having associated herself with the Ursuline Sisters.   Before the unlucky days she has been the fiancée of a brave young officer, whose

family have befriended her, and, as the
curtain rises, he is trying to get a trace
of her whereabouts in one of the Seine
boats, where he believes her to be in
hiding under the guise of a washer-
woman's daughter. While pursuing his
search—seemingly a fruitless one—he
runs across a former college mate whom
he has not seen for years, and while he
is taking him into his confidence regarding *Fabienne* the young girl comes
running towards him, followed by a
crowd of angry women and men, who
accuse her of being an aristocrat.
Martial, her lover, essays to protect
her, but in vain. The crowd will not
listen to reason. She is one of the
noblesse and a *suspecte*. They continue
their persecutions, and it is only when
Martial's old friend and comrade un-
buttons his coat and shows the badge
of an Agent of Public Safety, as the

Republican guards were then called, that the crowd falls back and permits them to pass unmolested.

The next scene is in the house of a good woman, a friend of *Labussière's* (who is the agent above referred to), *Mme. Berillon. Labussière* guides his new-found friend and his protégée here for a place of refuge. A conversation ensues, in which *Labussière* learns that *Fabienne* has drawn on her head the wrath of a former stable hand of her father's, now grown into revolutionary prominence, to whom she applied for protection. He was in a state of brutal intoxication, and denounced her, whereupon she fled from him in terror, and he in revenge accused her of trying to assassinate him. *Labussière* realises her danger, questions them both, and advises them to get passports, change their costumes, and fly to Belgium without delay.

The scene is an interesting one. *Martial* and *Fabienne* are seized with horror on learning *Labussière's* occupation ; but when he tells them his reasons for being in the service, it is justifiable in their eyes. It is, he says, to save the innocent. He was himself condemned, but saved to become Executor of the Decrees. His first authorisation was directed against his benefactor, to save whom he destroyed the warrant, and escaped punishment by pretending to be a silly and careless fellow, and to have misplaced it. By one subterfuge and another he then managed to cheat the scaffold daily of many victims.

While they are talking an agent comes and announces the probable overthrow and arrest of *Robespierre*, and *Labussière* and *Martial* hasten out— the one to verify the news, the other to secure passports to Belgium. Before

Martial leaves, however, he takes occasion to renew his suit to *Fabienne*, and begs her to accept his hand as she has always had his heart. *Fabienne* is in agony. While in the convent, and under the impression that *Martial* was dead, she has taken preliminary vows, and she considers herself bound to complete them. *Martial* reasons with her, and finally induces her to relinquish this idea and consent to fly with him. In the meantime, *Fabienne* has sent a messenger to the Ursuline Convent. He returns breathless with the news that the convent is invaded and the Sisters condemned to death—even now they are passing the door. The letter has been taken from the messenger, and while *Fabienne* opens the window to take a last look at her beloved friends, while she is absorbed in emotion and remorse, the door is thrown open and an agent enters in search of her, whom he suspects of being one of the Sisters. "Who are you?" he asks.

"*Fabienne Lecoulteux*, an Ursuline Sister!"

"You are arrested?" *Fabienne* is taken to the Conciérgérie.

The third act is the strongest in the play. It takes place in a partly dismantled room of the Tuileries turned into a council-room. *Labussière* and *Martial* are excitedly discussing a means to secure *Fabienne's* release, and prompt action is necessary. It is impossible, as heretofore, to destroy the order—it has been made too important, and is the one case before the tribunal of interest, owing to the accusation of attempted assassination of a high official—the ex-stableman. Nothing remains but to put in a substitute. The name is common, and there are several accused who could take her place; but *Labussière*, who has only saved lives, hesitates to take one and to become a murderer. File after file they turn over, and one reason and another prevents their taking advantage of each and every one. No, they cannot sacrifice a life by putting in a substitute. While they are seeking a means a courier comes with the news that *Robespierre* is overthrown, and all the leaders arrested, including *Fabienne's* accuser. "Then she is free," cries *Martial*, and both start for the Conciérgérie as cries of "Vive la Republique!" resound, and *Robespierre* and his accomplices file past in the hands of the jailors.

The fourth and last act is in the court of the Conciérgérie. The Black Van is already waiting at the usual hour to convey the victims of the guil-

lotine as *Labussière* and *Martial* arrive.
The crowd is great, and rumours of all
sorts fill the air. *Robespierre* is re-
ported arrested, when suddenly the re-
port is contradicted on authority.. The
agents, fearing their heads may pay
the penalty of a failure to go on with
the executions, begin calling the names
of the unfortunates, who come forward
to take their places in the van. *Labussière* is in despair. At last he
thinks of a way to save *Fabienne*—
there is a respite for women who are
about to become mothers. Making
himself known to the agent, he secures
the customary document, which only
needs *Fabienne's* signature to effect her
release. As she appears she is un-
conscious of the nature of the paper,
and in her bewilderment she takes the
pen in hand, but recoils in horror at
signing her own infamy. Entreaties

are of no avail. Not even the hope of release can influence her. She refuses. She is being led away, when *Martial*, who can stand it no longer, attacks the agent. Foolish lover! His death pays the penalty; he is instantly shot, and expires as his fiancée is being taken to the scaffold.

She utters a cry as the van moves, and the curtain falls on Sardou's sublime work.

This is a faint outline of the plot, which but little expresses its intensity or grandeur. The play, to be appreciated, must be seen as well as read. As an illustration of the greatest moral lesson in the history of the world, the French Revolution, it has a higher purpose than was accredited in the treatment it received at the hands of the Comédie Française audience. The moral is against the state of society which made such friends of men that they sacrifice the lives of thousands of innocent *Fabiennes* for the maintenance of "*liberté, egalité, et fraternité.*" As to where the responsibility lies for that state of society, even philosophical historians have failed to agree.

The original French cast included :

JOLIBON (coiffeur) . . .	MME. BOUCHER
BERILLON (lampiste)	GARRAUD.
Un Pecheur a la Ligne . .	LELOIR.
RIBOUT (employé de Comité de Salut public) . . .	JOLIET.
WOLF (Commis-Greffier du Tribunal)	DUPONT-VERNON.
BRAULT (Conciérge de la Conciérgérie). . . .	ROGER.
POURVOYEUR (éspion) . .	VILLAIN.
CHATEUIL (employé du Comité de Salut Public) . .	SAMARY.
BRICART	CLERH.
SAMSON (Bourreau) . . .	FALCONNIER.
BOUCHART (Mémbre de la Section de l'Arsenal) . .	HAMEL.
OLIVON (employé à la Conciérgérie)	GRAVOLLET.
MARTEAU (Secrétaire du Bureau de Police) . . .	PIERRE LAUGIER.

TAVERNIER (Huissier du Tribunnal).	MME. GEORGES BEER.
DEBURN (Lieutenant de Gendarmérie	LEITNER.
VASSELIN ·(employé du Comité de Salut Public) . .	COCHERIS.
GASPARD (petit commis de Berillon)	DEHELLY.
CHARLES LABUSSIÈRE . .	COQUELIN.
MARTIAL HUGON . . .	MARAIS.
LUPIN (petit commis du Bureau des Détenus) . . .	JEAN COQUELIN.
FABIENNE LECOULTEUX . .	MLLE. BARTET.
LA MARIOTTE	MLLE. AMEL.
JACQUELINE (femme de Berillon)	E. HADAMARD.
MLLE. BRAULT	LUDWIG.
FRANÇOISE	LYNNES.

MM. CH. ESQUIER, FORDYCE, JACQUES, FENOUX,
FRANCK, GAULEY, RAVET.

It is strange that, of all the countries in the universe, it remains to the United States to be the one to fittingly produce the great French author's work. Charles Frohman, the indefatigable projector (by a strange coincidence styled the Napoleon of Managers), has mounted the play in a manner befitting and even surpassing the Comédie Française production. Mr, Frohman has always had faith in the drawing qualities of Sardou's works in America, and it suits the broadness of his plans to interest himself in productions of great magnitude, so that he was undaunted by the difficulties in " Thermidor." Being in direct communication with M. Sardou, he has been enabled to take advantage of his suggestions and almost hourly interest in the play. So interested is M. Sardou, that in a recent interview he expressed the hope and expectation that the Americans would revenge him for the ill-treatment he received in Paris. The negotiations for the presentation were successfully carried on by Miss Elizabeth Marbury, who has the honour to represent M. Sardou in America and Mr. Charles Frohman in Europe.

In Miss Elsie Anderson de Wolfe, who makes her début on the professional stage, will be seen a *Fabienne* of typical grace and inherited qualifications. She is, in one sense, an artistic foster-child of the author, and better fitted for the rôle on this account than a more experienced artist might be. She is tall, *svelte* and *brune*, with the dark eyes and characteristic mien of a daughter of the French aristocracy. She looks the rôle to perfection, and only needs to appear to put the finishing touch to the ideality of the production. M. Sardou is also personally interested in her success.

The opinions of the London press on the original production are subjoined, as being the only ones sufficiently just and impartial to reproduce; the French criticisms (from the moment the play was judged from a political standpoint) being notoriously opinionated and biassed.

AT THE THÉÂTRE FRANÇAISE.

OPINIONS OF THE LONDON PRESS.

TIMES.

"REALISM has never been brought to greater perfection. The howling of the mob, the tocsin, the revolting sayings and jests are marvellously depicted. An epoch cannot be more strikingly and faithfully delineated. The piece is a denunciation of the Terror which even now finds a few defenders, and perhaps would-be repeaters; but there is nothing new in this indictment, and this violent declamation is scarcely consistent with calm severity of history. I have intentionally omitted to speak of M. Coquelin's rôle, though his constant intervention fills the piece, though he acts with wonderful perfection. Mlle. Bartet, as *Fabienne*, shows much dignity and emotion. M. Marais, as *Martial*, is too melodramatic, and one could understand the cry from the gallery on the fall of the curtain "A l'Ambigu!" Still, it is well that the piece has been brought out at the Française, for nowhere else would it have been so admirably mounted and acted."

"There is much dialogue at the beginning of each of the first three acts, which might be thought excessive on any other stage than that of the Comédie Française, and the scene between *Labussière* and *Martial* in the Third Act is protracted so long as to become almost painful; but every act concludes with an exciting scene worked to a climax with extraordinary dramatic skill.   But the finest effect of the piece is unquestionably that of the Second Act, where the Sisters are being carried off to prison. The impression is greater than it would be if we actually saw the procession, and M. Sardou has here repeated a means of procedure which served him in such good stead in the "torture scene" of "La Tosca." The acting in "Thermidor" is throughout as fine as can be imagined. In *Labussière* M. Coquelin has a part which suits him "down to the ground." Generally full of humour, but often terribly in earnest; deceiving his comrades by his assumption of imbecility, and astonishing his friends by his fertility of resource; the character of the real actor in the revolutionary drama gave the great artist of the Française opportunities for displaying his versatility of which he availed himself to the fullest possible extent. In the scene where *Labussière* refuses to sacrifice an unknown victim, M. Coquelin rose to tragic intensity. No more perfect ideal of the high-born, high-bred *Fabienne* can be imagined than Mlle. Bartet, who displayed unexpected emotional passion in the scene where she consents to forget her "vows." The *Martial* was M. Marais, who has evidently profited by M. Sardou's counsels, and justified the author's choice. To name all the characters—whereof there are nearly thirty—is out of the question, but mention should be made of Mlle. Hadamard, who was quite charming as the kind-hearted *costumière;* Mlle. Lynnes, who was a splendidly exuberant *tricôteuse;* and M. Jean Coquelin, who made a hit in the small part of *Lupin*, *Labussière's* faithful assistant. The peculiarity of the performance was that every one of the numerous *dramatis personæ* was perfect in his or her own line, and that all acted in the most natural way in the world. Here M. Sardou's consummate knowledge of the stage and unceasing solicitude for reality in the *mise en scène* were manifest. Needless to say that every scene, every uniform, and every costume was copied strictly from the drawings of the time, while even the cups and saucers were authentic. "Thermidor," as a literary exercitation, is a synthesis of the history of the Revolution : as it is put on the stage, it is a complement of the Musée Carnavalet.

MORNING POST.

Never, perhaps, has the genius of M. Sardou, as playwright and *metteur en scène*, been more remarkably displayed than in this production. He transports his audience as if by magic into the middle of the life of Paris just a hundred years ago. The tranquil Seine, in the first tableau, with its wooden bridge framed in poplar trees, and in the distance the towers of Notre Dame, is a marvel of poetic realism. In the modest apartment of *Berillon* the dressing-woman, what neatness and repose, and what a picture it gives us of the tranquil, honest life which must have passed along, almost undisturbed by the boisterous events and horrible street

tragedies of the Reign of Terror. In the
bureau of *Labussière*, in the Pavilion de Flore,
the most conscientious attention has been
paid to detail, and one could almost imagine
one's self in a salon of the Prefecture. The
tarnished glories of the former regal palace
are still partially visible. The vast mirror is
cracked, and a Republican proclamation
pasted over the broken glass. Piles and piles
of *dossiers* are heaped up against the gaudily
tinted walls, from which the *fleur de lys* still
stares out from an escutcheon high enough to
have escaped the general wreck. Equally
perfect is the scene at the conciérgérie with
its brightly dressed but sinister-looking mob,
flaunting Republican ribbons and colours,
and howling the ditties of the Revolution.

As to the acting, it is impossible to speak
in sufficiently high terms of M. Coquelin as
Labussière, of Mlle. Bartet as *Fabienne*, and
M. Marais as *Hugon*. They acted up to the
very best traditions of the French stage. The
remainder of the cast, a very lengthy one, was
in every respect excellent. Seldom has so
great a success been obtained at the Théâtre
Français, and M. Jules Claretie and M. Sar-

dou, both of whom are enthusiastic students of the great Revolutionary period, are to be congratulated upon the production of a piece which brings back, better perhaps than any history could do, the dreadful scenes of the Reign of Terror. From first to last it is a series of phantoms—terrible phantoms; and the fall of the curtain brings a sense of relief like the awakening from a nightmare.

DAILY CHRONICLE.

"Thermidor" might not inappropriately be called "Twenty-four Hours of the Reign of Terror." All the hideous events and fierce savagery of those ten months seem compressed in the incidents and dialogue. But the hands of the clock only go round twice, and the play itself is a pathetic and tragic love-story, growing up like a flower in a soil watered with the blood of thousands of victims.

The acting of the elder Coquelin as *Labussière* was admirable, and he was ably seconded by M. Marais, who is losing some of the rough angles caused by that want of training which the House of Molière has

given him. In the Third Act the two come-
dians—one impassioned and forgetful, the
other sad, indeed, but mindful and humane—
were well matched. The love scene of the
Second Act, between Mlle. Bartet and M.
Marais, was intensely powerful, and the delicate and refined actress has once more shown
herself at the top of her profession in the
delineation of subdued and poetic love. The
cast is a long one, and all the minor parts
were acted with that zeal and precision which
is only found at the Comédie Française.
"Thermidor" does not call for much "scenic
display," but as usual Sardou has shown himself a thoroughgoing stage manager, and the
production bears the impress of his personal
superintendence. It only remains to be seen
whether the dominant note of gloomy pathos
will militate against the run of the piece. All
one can say to-day is, that the illustrious playwright has once more gone into the paths
which led him to fame and fortune.

STANDARD.

The political bias which was so strongly
apparent in M. Sardou's "Rabagas" is, to

use a French idiom, very much "accentuated" in his new production, and as there are people still living in Paris who are powerful enough to raise statues to *Danton*, and to make out *Marat* to be an injured innocent, it is hardly to be wondered at that his exposure of the miserable cowardice which allowed a wretched gang of unscrupulous ruffians to send daily to the scaffold for nearly two years, not only the élite of the French people, but also the lowly and humble, should give rise to controversies. One of the critics exclaims that " La Comédie Française a commis un mauvaise action." Others point out that the play bears striking analogy to Alexandre Dumas the Elder's " Chevalier de Maison Rouge," and that M. Sardou was also haunted by a reminiscence of M. Ronan's " Abbesse de Jouarre."

The applause was enthusiastic at the fall of the curtain, but there were some shouts of " A l'Ambigu," intimating an opinion that the play, from its very melodramatic character, is more suited to the Boulevard theatres than to the classic boards of the Maison de Molière. The play is likely to have a tremendous run, not only from its sensational character, but also from the political element with which it is largely tinged, and the controversy to which it has, even at this early stage of its existence, begun to give rise. M. Ferry and a number of political notabilities were present.

SARAH BERNHARDT

AND SOME OF SARDOU'S ENGLISH
INTERPRETERS

LONDON has at last seen "Thermidor,"
and with one or two exceptions may be
said to have seen a very fine production
of the play. Coquelin has never been
in better form ; and his *Labussière* was
a marvel of artistic grace, strength,
and finish. He is so great, so consummate an artist, that beside him most
actors appear inexperienced amateurs:
by that I mean those actors or actresses
who play in an immediate cast with
him, and whose finest points only
serve to demonstrate the perfection of
his simplest effects. The quietness, the
elegance, the dignity of M. Coquelin put

his best companions to shame, and it is no more fair to judge them under these circumstances, than to despise electricity because it is not the sun.

Mlle. Jeanne Malvau as *Fabienne* succeeded Mlle. Bartet—la delicieuse Bartet—as Sardou styled her; and while Mlle. Malvau lacks those special qualifications which distinguished her French predecessor, she is still a young artist of excellent parts, her voice, school, and technique being those of the very first Parisian training and style. She was very effective, very strong, in the last reprise of Dora at the Paris Gymnase two seasons ago, and great things were expected of her. The future will show how these expectations are to be fulfilled, as I do not judge her alone by her performance in "Thermidor," although for so young an artist the latter was certainly very good.

The daily press has said so much

about the play, and has criticised it so liberally, so impartially, that I do not feel justified in adding my personal appreciation of it. But one thing strikes me as a remarkable proof of Sardou's vitality, versatility, and indispensability : at one present moment in London alone three theatres were playing Sardou—the Royal English Opera, the Opera Comique, and the Theatre Royal, Haymarket. The plays —"Cleopatra," "Peril" (the English version of " Nos Intimes"), and " Thermidor"—the much-discussed "Thermidor ;" the great Sarah Bernhardt as " Cleopatra," the great Coquelin as " Labussière," and the great English artist, H. Beerbohm Tree, as " Sir Woodbine Grafton."

A word here for this splendid actor, who for several years past has added not a little to the immense success of

the French master's plays in England—
his Sir Woodbine Grafton in " Peril,"
his Count Orloff in " Dora " (Diplomacy), are studies of such artistic
perfection that one never tires of seeing
them repeated. The great delight in
watching Beerbohm Tree is to note the
unfolding of the dramatic intellect, the
intellectual power brought to bear upon
each and every dramatic study, and the
marvellous intelligence of a nature that
is always striving to improve itself.
This quality would delight M. Sardou
as it does all thinking people, and is
one of those which he so adores in the
" Divine Sarah." That restlessness of
dramatic instinct, that kaleidoscope of
dramatic sensations, that crucible of
dramatic emotions into which the actor
or actress compounds all the elements
of sensibility, enthusiasm, and genius ;
who acts for the sake of acting, who

hangs on the pivot of impulse the spur of the moment; and who, like the master himself, rushes one on with him to the very verge of the possible, the very abysm of the terrifying, the very gulf of all scenic and dramatic effort. With such qualities as these the artist raises mumming to the sculptor's art, and the dramatist to that enduring fame whose confine may be reality, but whose broad expanse is living humanity.

I cite, almost at random, other English artists who have shone pre-eminent in the Sardouan drama. I first name that exquisite actress, Mrs. Kendall, in "A Scrap of Paper"— "Pattes de Mouche"—and in "Nos Intimes"—"Peril"; delightful in both rôles, and not outdone in any manner by her French sisters. Mrs. Bernard-Beere, magnificent in every way as

Feodora, and whose English creation
of the part at the Haymarket, directly
after its Parisian success, is still a
favourite there with amateurs of that
play. Mr. Forbes Robertson in " Diplomacy " and " Peril," an artist of the
most beautiful style and perfect school ;
Maurice Barrymore, the American *jeune
premier*, whose performance with Mr.
Bancroft and Forbes Robertson in the
famous man's trio of "Diplomacy,"
brought tears to every eye, and will
long be remembered as one of the most
remarkable and pathetic bits of acting
done in modern days. The Bancrofts
—names very dear to every Anglo-
Saxon heart — in both plays above
named, absolute perfection ; Miss Grace
Hawthorne, the American actress, a
splendid and surprising Theodora ; and
Mr. Murray Carson, a young actor of
romantic drama, whose Justinien was a

very remarkable study—full of power, finesse, and dramatic insight ; Chas. Brookfield, the Robertsons one and all, the Terrys, John Hare, the Kendalls, and so many more English artists I cannot name them, constitute a galaxy of Anglo-Saxon artists to whom, were M. Sardou to give but one sole hand-shake, his wrist would ache more than that of the President of the United States after his first New Year's reception in the White House, when all his electors' families, with their sisters and their cousins and their aunts, come up to the Capitol to say " Hail to the Chief," and to wish him—ah ! more dramatic souvenirs—Rip Van Winkle's toast—Well, here's a health to you and your families, and may you all live long and prosper.

We now arrive at the latest triumphs of the maître, the Bernhardt season at

the Royal English Opera House, where
the famed artist at present writing
daily packs one of the largest theatres
in London with all that is fashionable,
artistic, and cultivated of the great
metropolis. The greatest nights are
when " La Tosca," " Cleopatra," and
" Fedora " are given—more Sardou—
and the town seems absolutely running wild with enthusiasm. The
management have spared no expense,
and the opening performance of the
season—" Cleopatra "—was a surprise
to every one, not alone for the correctness and beauty of the stage fittings,
but for the general excellence of the
company—far above the usual aver-
age support given to celebrated stars.
Amongst the best artists are Mes-
dames Mea, Fleury, Simonson ; MM.
Deschamps and Rebel ; and last, but
not least, M. Albert Darmont, a very

young actor and author, whose fire, enthusiasm, and intelligence lent unusual
charm to the rôle of Marc Antony, and
who ably seconded the great comédienne
in delineating this ever-fascinating scenio-
love tale.

Is there anything left to say of this
remarkable woman, whose proper bio-
graphy cannot be amiss in a life of
Sardou ?   Of all his interpreters he
owes the most to her.   She is identi-
fied with all his last works, and owes
to the dramatist her most brilliant and
lasting triumphs.   Moreover, she has
never played as she is playing now,
and that, too, immediately after a
tournée round the world of a length
and fatigue probably unknown to any
other living actress.   She never gives
a bad performance, and, frankly, when
one listens to " La Tosca " in the after-
noon, and to " Fedora " the same even-

ing, one cannot but marvel at such
human endurance, and, were it necessary or possible, would be quite willing to forgive any laxity of the
artist's resisting powers ; no matter
what she does, one can only say,
"How astonishing! How wonderful!
How delightful ! "

One day, discussing her, Sardou
said :

"The world thinks it knows Sarah
Bernhardt—that it has an adequate idea
of her genius, her resources, her intelligence ; but it is wrong. It has absolutely no conception of what she is
capable—of her fertility, her quickness,
her terrific capacity of seizing upon
the idea of the author, of instantly
executing and carrying out, not alone
what he has written, but what he
originally thought and would have
written, had he been able. In order

to appreciate this, one must see her daily at rehearsals, must know her inner life, must come upon her at odd moments, when she is not the artist, but the woman, and—mon Dieu !—what a woman ! Always inventive, ready, sympathetic ; a generosity of disposition ahead of any human being I have ever met ; always giving everything away, helping sister artists — poor artists, any one, every one, artist or not, who comes in her way, and makes appeal to her heart.

"She is just like her father, patterned of him and after him ; a man with le diable au corps, never quiet a moment ; always interesting, always gay, always en train. The two together are something absolutely unique, and go to one's head like a strong wine. Ah ! je l'aime bien allez, ·la grande Sarah !—et l'on peut bien s'immaginer le plaisir d'écrire

pour une créature pareille. Je voudrais
qui tout le monde la connaisse comme
je la connais—et on verra bien que de
toutes les éloges qu'on lui a faites, on en
saurait jamais dire assez—et on en a
pas encore fait assez."

Sardou may rave in French, but as
it is not so easy for me, I shall do my
raving in English ; and perhaps I have
already raved enough, only I always
seem to see her as I saw her long ago—
the delicious Sarah Bernhardt, of the
Comedie Française, set in its wonderful frame of artists, herself the gem—
all too worthy of even the finest setting ;
a picture of which our days shall probably not see the like again, here,
there, or anywhere.

She was playing "La Fille de
Roland," a strange study of French
life and manners, but the one I think
which first revealed Sarah Bernhardt

to the world, an inspired creature, of beauty, genius, grace, and charm, whom I see, as then, standing at the window ; fair hair crowning the white forehead, eyes blue with that mystic blue of the distant mountain, a face like the sphynx, a smile like the dawn, teeth like orient pearl, a skin of marble purity, a figure like that of a child, and a voice—a voice, once heard, whose gold for ever rings in the ears : whose accents linger like perfume on the air, and whose perfect melody is one of those extra-ordinary gifts Nature alone is responsible for.

Like the Serpent of the Nile, " age cannot wither nor custom stale her infinite variety "; years have passed, seasons have been born, have blossomed, have died, but she alone has not changed. She is Cleopatra ; she is La Tosca ; she is Feodora ; but she is always and ever—La Bernhardt; the greatest actress of her time; the most wonderful woman; the one, the fascinating, the unique—Sarah Bernhardt.

SARDOU

AND now this little memoir of the great author is to be closed by none other than the Dramatist himself. The cruel and terrible Franco-Prussian war furnishes the epoch, Paris the *mise en scène*, and the episode was:

COMMENT J'AI PRIS LES TUILERIES*
BY VICTORIEN SARDOU.

I was following the stream of eager spectators who pressed along the Rue Royale to the Chambre des Deputés. They were dispersed by a crowd going in the opposite direction which suddenly

---

* From the original French.—B.R.

invaded the Boulevards, spreading such scraps of news as: "The Chambre no longer exists!" "The Empire has been proclaimed." "General Trochu is constructing a temporary Government at the Hôtel de Ville."

These different announcements thrown among the crowd awoke neither joy nor indignation, but were accepted with that kind of dazed stupidity which had been visible since the preceding day upon all faces, and which plainly signified, "What does it matter? Nothing will surprise us after Sedan!"

There were few people on the Place de la Concorde—most of the curious had already gone to the Hôtel de Ville —by the quays and the Rue de Rivoli.

The most conspicuous group was stationed in front of the Pont Tournant, trying to force open the gate. All the sentinels had disappeared. Amongst

K

these I saw Armand Gouzien, contemplating with upturned face an individual who, mounted on one of the pilasters, was fiercely beating the Golden Eagle of the Coronation with a heavy mallet. The eagle fell, striking one of the applauding spectators on the forehead.

The next moment the gate was broken down, and about 300 people, amongst them Gouzien and myself, penetrated into the garden. The remainder of the crowd wisely remained in the square; those even who had entered the gates grouped themselves in the open space between the two terraces without daring to venture so far as the fountain.

This sudden timidity had a cause. At the very moment when the gate had been burst open a detachment of the Imperial Guard was placed in front of the principal door of the Palace, and remained there, immovable, stolid, their guns in readiness.

Gouzien grasped my arm and whispered: "What is going to happen?"

"Bah!" I answered. "It's inevitable! A shot will be fired, the Guard will immediatety reply by stretching two or three men dead; these will be carried about the streets. Fire-arms will be brought out from every direction. The Tuileries will be besieged—the Guards will die, but not yield—but the palace will be taken, ransacked, burnt! I saw the assault of the Tuileries in '48—a grand spectacle—it does honour to the French nation. If we are to see such things again."

"And remember," said G., "that the flag is still waving up there, and that the Empress is still at the palace."

The spectators were getting more and more excited and agitated. After

the first movement of fear the crowd
seemed inclined to fight, and their num-
bers were visibly swelling.

"It is getting stormy," said Gouzien,
"and begins to smell of powder."

"Shall we try to save the Tuileries, you
and I together?" said I.

"Certainly; but how can we?"

"We can go and find out who is the
commanding officer, tell him to call
back the Guard, and in its place to put
the National Guards or the Mobiles;
the crowd will never fire on *them*, and
the palace will be saved!"

"True; but will these people give
us time to act?"

"Speak to them."

"Why don't you?"

"No; you are tall, fine-looking, and
will make more impression on them
than I could. But don't forget to call
them 'Citizens'!"

Gouzien called to his aid the finest tones of his voice, and, addressing the crowd, emitted a "Citizens!" which instantly had the effect of making all faces turn towards us.

"Citizens!" he repeated, "you are justly angered that this garden is not open to all, and that armed forces prevent you from entering—(Murmurs of assent). The Revolution has been declared, and consequently the people have the right to enter the Tuileries because the Tuileries belong to them!—(Great applause). Since the Empire no longer exists, the presence of the Imperial Guard is quite out of season—(Bravo! Bravo!) Therefore we propose, Citizen Sardou and I, to go and demand the withdrawal of these soldiers—(Tremendous effect). Only, you must give us your word not to move before our return— think what disastrous consequences a single shot even in mistake may have. Do nothing which may give rise to a misunderstanding, but wait here quietly till we return.

This proposition was received with great applause.

" Yes, yes. Go ! go ! We will wait here for you ! "

" Let's be off," I said to Gouzien ; and, followed by the curious looks of all those people we marched along the broad avenue in the direction of the palace.

The position was so novel and un-expected that we walked for some moments in silence, full of emotion. The Grand Allée stretched before us deserted and scorched by the burning sun ; and the soldiers who from a dis-tance saw our two poor little shadows walking alone in this large bare space towards the palace, like two ants going to storm a milestone, were no doubt

wondering "what we were up to now."
The thought suddenly struck us that
they might possibly take a wrong view
of the proceeding, and unconsciously we
drifted little by little from the centre of
the Allée to the right, and were prepared to take refuge behind the trunk
of a tree at the first alarming symptom.
A very marked movement now taking
place in the front ranks made us decide
upon enlightening the squadron as to
our pacific intentions.

"Perhaps it would be better," suggested Gouzien, "to show them that we
are here as bearers of a flag of truce."

"Just what I was thinking of," said
I; and pulling my handkerchief from
my pocket, I tied it to my stick, thus
making a little flag. Gouzien having
done likewise, we returned to the middle
of the broad path, our fears somewhat
tranquillised. It was then that we

were joined by a lieutenant of the Garde Mobile, who had till then followed us prudently under the shelter of the trees, and who came, he assured us, to take part in our generous action. He was rather coldly welcomed, as the presence of his uniform seemed to alter the character of our embassy.

At last we reached the end of the Grande Allée, then we passed the flower-beds, and walked round the fountain which is just before the entrance to the private garden. Then I looked behind towards the Place de la Concorde, and there I saw our people grouped near the Grand Bassin : they were keeping their promise. We were now only a few steps from the gate of the private garden—it was closed. In front of us the Guards stood motionless ; only a few officers were passing to and fro ; then suddenly two black coats appeared—an old keeper with grey whiskers came forward, followed by two younger ones, and they reached the gate at the very moment when we stopped before it.

"What do you want?" he asked gruffly.

The welcome was rather displeasing, and the good man's zeal seemed to us rather uncalled for. We replied quietly that our business was not with him, but with the officer in command of the palace.

" General Mellinet?"

" Ah!" cried Gouzien, "is it General Mellinet? I am glad to hear that—he knows me. Please go and tell him that we beg to have the honour of speaking with him—MM. Victorien Sardou and Armand Gouzien. Here are our cards!"

The man, to whom our names were not quite unknown, though he did not feel sure if they were not those of two rogues, took the cards and then turned :

" Here is the General ! "

Then we saw the General coming to us with a gentleman in a frock-coat. This coat, I only heard later on, belonged to M. de Lesseps, whom, strange to say. I did not know, and whom I met then for the first time.

The General seemed very much upset and in a rage.

" What do you want, gentlemen ? " cries he, after rapidly glancing at our cards. " I have made a promise, and *I* will keep it ! "

His anger had a cause, and the *I* was very expressive. The brave General had just heard that Trochu, who was expected at the Tuileries, was at that moment at the Hotel de Ville.

" General," said Gouzien, " there is

no question of breaking your promise—
far from it. Your duty is to defend the
Tuileries."

"Yes, sir, and I will do so!"

Here the lieutenant of the Mobiles
broke in, and exclaimed that the
Tuileries belonged to the people, and
the people.

It was Gouzien's own speech, but
though very good at one end of the
Tuileries, it would be the reverse at the
other end. We hurriedly cut it short,
fearing lest it should spoil all. I cried:
"General, we desire nothing better than
that you should save the palace. But
if you can do so without causing the
death of a single man, you won't be
sorry, will you?"

"No, certainly."

"Well," said Gouzien, "let us show
you the way to do so; but tell us first,
is the Empress still in the palace?"

" No ; she has just left it."

"Then, General, lower the flag. Then put the National Guard or the Mobiles in the place of the Imperial Guard ! And then you may be sure that the palace will not be injured ! "

The General thought it over—those around seemed to approve our counsel.

" I see nothing against what you advise—I have some of the National Guard at the Place Vendôme and some Mobiles at the Carrousel, both near at hand. I prefer the Mobiles."

" More especially," said Gouzien, "as they are nearer, and time is very precious."

It was so. Already during this conversation the aspect of things had changed behind us. While we came along the avenue a good number of the curious had followed at a distance by a side march under shelter of the trees. They had stopped near the Quincunxes to watch the effect of our proposal. As soon as they saw us in conference with uniforms they understood that all fear of firing was over, and, coming into the full glare of the sun, they advanced towards us rapidly. Gaining confidence the greater number of the crowd, who had remained at the Pont Tournant, started also in the same direction. In a few minutes the whole lot would join us. The General gave his commands rapidly. The only question now remaining to be decided was whether the Garde Mobile or the crowd would be up first.

"In such a case, General, there is only one resource—speak to all these people, and amuse them, so as to give the Mobiles time to come up.".

"A chair!" cried the General. A

keeper rushed forward and brought one
from under some trees.

" Gentlemen," said the General, standing on the chair, " the palace is empty
—the Empress is no longer there.
But it is my duty to protect the Tuileries,
and to accomplish this proposal I count
upon your civility, the wisdom of the
people, &c." And other rigmaroles which
the General strung off very cleverly, but
in which he believed no more than the
people who were listening to him. I
was not listening : one thought only
preoccupied me—the Mobiles were a
long time coming. The General's speech
was beginning to fall rather flat, when
suddenly the Imperial Guard moved
away. Their departure was received with
a great clamour ; the people imagined
themselves already masters of the
Tuileries. At the same moment the
Mobiles came from the hall, running

also, with their bayonets in front of them, and stationed themselves in two rows between the palace and the gardens, as though their only object were to prevent the devastation of the gardens. The General jumped off his chair and moved away with Gouzien. The gate was flung open, and the flood of invaders rushed to the palace, which seemed to be opened to them ; they sprang up the steps, rushed into the vestibule with shouts of joy ; but there and everywhere they found the two rows of Guards, leaving between them only a large passage with a hedge of guns on either side. Carried on by their impetuosity and obliged to go straight forward to the door, our brawlers found themselves on the other side of the palace in the Carrousel, and were both astonished and disappointed : they understood at last that they had been duped, and walked off pitifully, their hands in their pockets. Their game was spoilt!

Then, thinking that Gouzien and I had not lost any time, I lit a cigarette and turned round to go back the way I came.

And I found myself face to face with a good-for-nothing rascal, who leered maliciously at me and said :

" Ah ! deuce take you ! What did you want to put your finger in our pie for—eh ? "

FINIS